The Message Of Salvation

Basic Scriptural and Liturgical Teaching in Christian Living for the Millions of Unchurched Americans, for Our Brethren in any way Separated from the Catholic Church and for Modern Catholics.

by FATHER FARRELL

FARE, INC.
794 Pearson Street
Des Plaines, Illinois 60016

PERMISSIONS

Prayers by Lawrence Dannemiller originally appeared in the book, *Reading the Word of God*, ©1960 by Lawrence Dannemiller. Permission to use these prayers was granted by the publisher, Helicon Press, Inc., Baltimore, Maryland.

Excerpts from The Jerusalem Bible, copyrighted 1966 by Darton, Longman & Todd, Ltd. and Doubleday & Company, Inc. Used by permission of the publishers.

Excerpts from The Constitutions, Decrees, and Declarations of the Ecumenical Council are taken from The Documents of Vatican II, published by Guild Press, America Press, Association Press, and Herder and Herder, and copyrighted 1966 by the America Press. Used by permission.

Excerpts from the Ritual approved by the National Conferences of Bishops of the United States of America, published by Benziger Bros., Inc., copyrighted 1964 by the National Catholic Welfare Conference, are used by permission of N. C. W. C.

Excerpts from the New Experimental Funeral Rite are used by permission of the Liturgy Training Program, the Confraternity of Christian Doctrine, Chicago, Illinois.

NIHIL OBSTAT: Reverend Edmund Siedlecki
Censor Deputatus

IMPRIMATUR: Rt. Rev. Msgr. Francis W. Byrne
Vicar General, Archdiocese of Chicago

DATE: April 23, 1968
Revised Edition: 1971

The Nihil Obstat and Imprimatur are official declarations that a book or pamphlet is free of doctrinal or moral error. No implication is contained therein that those who have granted the Nihil Obstat and Imprimatur agree with the contents, opinions or statements expressed.

Fare, Inc.
794 Pearson Street
Des Plaines, Illinois 60016

THE KERYGMA: THE MESSAGE OF THIS BOOK

To bring God and His Message to our brethren not full members of The Catholic Church is the aim of this book. The sincere seeker is best led to the God of Salvation in the depth and beauty of Holy Scripture. Through Jesus Christ His Son Our Lord union with God is effected in our rich Catholic liturgy.

Reverend Martin Farrell

OUR CHRISTIAN PROCLAMATION TO YOU

Something which has existed since the beginning, that we have heard, and we have seen with our own eyes; that we have watched and touched with our hands: the Word, Who is life—this is our subject. That life was made visible: we saw it and we are giving our testimony, telling you of the eternal life which was with the Father and has been made visible to us. What we have seen and heard we are telling you so that you too may be in union with us, as we are in union with the Father and with His Son Jesus Christ. We are writing this to you to make our own joy complete. 1 Jn 1:1-4

The Message

Lesson Page

GOD OUR FATHER

JESUS CHRIST THE SON OF GOD

UNION WITH GOD THROUGH HIS CHURCH

Of Salvation

God Our Father

Lesson 1: GOD LOVES YOU

1. God Loves You

God loves you. God always has loved you and always will love you. He has loved you from the moment He thought of your creation. He will love you for all eternity. God can speak of His love for you as He spoke of His love for His Chosen People, the Jews, in the Old Testament: *I have loved you with an everlasting love, so I am constant in My affection for you.* Jr 31:3

St. John tells us of the depth of God's love for each individual:

> Yes, God loved the world so much that He gave His only Son, so that everyone who believes in Him may not be lost but may have eternal life. For God sent His Son into the world not to condemn the world, but so that through Him the world might be saved. No one who believes in Him will be condemned; but whoever refuses to believe is condemned already, because he has refused to believe in the name of God's only Son. Jn 3:16-18

Because God loves you and every human being with an undying deep love St. John goes so far as to call God love: *My dear people, let us love one another since love comes from God and everyone who loves is begotten by God and knows God. Anyone who fails to love can never have known God, because God is love.* 1 Jn 4:7-8

2. God Loves You As An Individual

You might be surprised to realize that God loves you as an individual person as if you were the only person in existence, in the same way that your father loves you, not only as a part of your family, but as a distinct member of your family. You should apply the words of this beautiful Psalm to yourself:

> Yahweh is my shepherd, I lack nothing. In meadows of green grass He lets me lie. To the waters of repose He leads me; there He revives my soul. He guides me by paths of virtue for the sake of His name. Though I pass through a gloomy valley, I fear no harm; beside me Your rod and Your staff are there, to hearten me. You prepare a table before me under the eyes of my enemies; You anoint my head with oil, my cup brims over. Ah, how goodness and kindness pursue me, every day

of my life; my home, the house of Yahweh, as long as I live! Ps 23:1-6

3. God Shows His Love For You By Giving You Life

Life is the most valuable gift of nature anyone can possess. The Scripture tells us: *Since it is in Him that we live, and move, and exist.* Ac 17:28

4. God Shows His Love For You By Watching Over You

God watches over you every moment of your existence. Every beat of your heart, every breath you take depends on God. For how many years has God been keeping you alive? For twenty years? For thirty years? For forty years? For fifty years? Each moment of that existence of yours depends on God.

God watches over you with a father's love: *Can you not buy two sparrows for a penny? And yet not one falls to the ground without your Father knowing. Why, every hair on your head has been counted. So there is no need to be afraid; you are worth more than hundreds of sparrows.* Mt 10:29-31. God is near you always. You can say to God and to God only: *But I put my trust in You, Yahweh, I say, "You are my God." My days are in Your hand, rescue me from the hands of my enemies and persecutors; let Your face smile on Your servant, save me in Your love.* Ps 31:14-16

5. God Shows His Love For You By Giving You So Many Gifts

God gave you all the good things in life that you have, your health, your wealth, your food, your family, your house, your friends; all are from the hand of the good God. After realizing how much God has given you, you should exclaim with St. Paul:

> How rich are the depths of God—how deep His wisdom and knowledge—and how impossible to penetrate His motives or understand His methods! Who could ever know the mind of the Lord? Who could ever be His counsellor? Who could ever give Him anything or lend Him anything? All that exists come from Him; all is by Him and for Him. To Him be glory for ever! Amen. Rm 11:33-36

Much of the evil in your life, especially sin, you acquire by your own efforts or by your own mistakes.

6. God Loves You Even When You Are In Sin

God is patient with you if you are a sinner because He realizes how weak you are. *The Lord . . . is being patient with you all, wanting nobody to be lost and everybody to be brought to change his ways.* 2 P 3:9. You should be as patient with yourself in sin as God is. Don't give up the idea of returning God's love. God's patience and mercy are greater than your sins: *As tenderly as a father treats his children, so Yahweh treats those who fear Him; He knows what we are made of, He remembers we are dust.* Ps 102:13-14

7. God Loves You So Much That He Will Forgive Your Sins

Through His immense love for you, God will forgive your sins, if you will repent: *As I live—it is the Lord Yahweh Who speaks—I take pleasure, not in the death of a wicked man, but in the turning back of a wicked man who changes his ways to win life.* Ezk 33:11 Isaiah made it clear: *Come now, let us talk this over, says Yahweh. Though your sins are like scarlet, they shall be as white as snow; though they are red as crimson, they shall be like wool.* Is 1:18. Repentance for your sins can bring to your heart the joy experienced by the Prodigal Son:

> He also said, "A man had two sons. The younger said to his father, 'Father, let me have the share of the estate that would come to me.' So the father divided the property between them. A few days later, the younger son got together everything he had and left for a distant country where he squandered his money on a life of debauchery. When he had spent it all, that country experienced a severe famine, and now he began to feel the pinch, so he hired himself out to one of the local inhabitants who put him on his farm to feed the pigs. And he would willingly have filled his belly with the husks the pigs were eating but no one offered him anything. Then he came to his senses and said, 'How many of my father's paid servants have more food than they want, and here am I dying of hunger! I will leave this place and go to my father and say: Father, I have sinned against heaven and against you; I no longer deserve to be called your son; treat me as one of your paid servants.' So he left the place and went back to his father. While he was still a long way off, his father saw him and was moved with pity. He ran to the boy, clasped him in his arms and kissed him tenderly. Then his son said, 'Father, I have sinned against heaven and against you. I no longer

deserve to be called your son.' But the father said to his servants, 'Quick! Bring out the best robe and put it on him; put a ring on his finger and sandals on his feet. Bring the calf we have been fattening, and kill it; we are going to have a feast, a celebration, because this son of mine was dead and has come back to life; he was lost and is found.' And they began to celebrate." Lk 15:11-24

8. God's Love For You Should Fill Your Heart With Joyful Reverence And Thankfulness And With A Desire To Love God In Return

Whenever a man thinks of God's immense love for him he ought to desire to love God in return. *Bless Yahweh, my soul, bless His Holy Name, all that is in me! Bless Yahweh, my soul, and remember all His kindnesses: in forgiving all your offenses, in curing all your diseases, in redeeming your life from the Pit, in crowning you with love and tenderness.* Ps 103:1-4

9. You Should Seek Union With God

The purpose of the training you will receive in this course of religious instructions is to lead you to union with God through love that leads to prayer. St. Luke tells us the purpose of our effort: *And He did this so that all nations might seek the deity and, by feeling their way towards Him, succeed in finding Him. Yet in fact He is not far from any of us, since it is in Him that we live, and move, and exist. . . .* Ac 17:27-28. Your life can be a new and joyous life with God. Remember, again, be patient with yourself; union with God is the final aim of our instructions and prayer. Union will not come quickly. *Set your hearts on His kingdom first, and on His righteousness, and all those other things will be given you as well.* Mt 6:33

10. You Depend On God Totally

From a realization of God's loving care for you, you must realize your total dependence upon God so that you must prayerfully say with King David, the author of the Book of Psalms: *My days are in Your hand,* Ps 31:15. St. Peter gives you good advice: *Bow down, then, before the power of God now, and He will raise you up on the appointed day; unload all your worries on to Him, since He is looking after you.* 1 P 5:6-7

11. Peace Be With You

The purpose of the course you are receiving from a parish priest or other instructor is not so much to impart a knowledge of God as it is to lead you to joyous union with God Who alone can give you peace and happiness. As you begin this course of religious instructions imagine Jesus Himself saying to you: *Peace I give to you, My own peace I give you, a peace the world cannot give, this is My gift to you.* Jn 14:27

CHRISTIAN PRACTICE

Sit quietly and try to count the blessings God has given you. Believe in God and trust in God all the days of your life as the inspired Word of God directs you in the 46th Psalm: *God is our shelter, our strength, ever ready to help in time of trouble, so we shall not be afraid when the earth gives way, when mountains tumble into the depths of the sea, and its waters roar and seethe, the mountains tottering as it heaves. Yahweh Sabaoth is on our side, our citadel, the God Jacob! There is a river whose streams refresh the city of God, and it sanctifies the dwelling of the Most High. God is inside the city, she can never fall, at crack of dawn God helps her; to the roaring of nations and tottering of kingdoms, when He shouts, the world disintegrates. Yahweh Sabaoth is on our side, our citadel, the God of Jacob! Come, think of Yahweh's marvels, the astounding things He has done in the world; all over the world He puts an end to wars, He breaks the bow, He snaps the spear, He gives shields to the flames. Pause a while and know that I am God, exalted among the nations, exalted over the earth! Yahweh Sabaoth is on our side, our citadel, the God of Jacob!*

CHRISTIAN PRAYER

Glory to God in the highest, and peace to His people on earth. Lord God, heavenly King, Almighty God and Father, we worship You, we give You thanks, we praise You for Your glory. Lord Jesus Christ, only Son of the Father, Lord God, Lamb of God, You take away the sins of the world: have mercy on us; You are seated at the right hand of the Father: receive our prayer. For You alone are the Holy One, You alone are the Lord, You alone are the Most High, Jesus Christ, with the Holy Spirit, in the glory of God the Father. Amen. *The Mass*

SUGGESTED READING FROM SCRIPTURE

Through this Revelation, therefore, the invisible God out of the abundance of His love speaks to men as friends and lives among them. *Second Vatican Council*

Mt 6:25-34 – Trust the Father.
Is 43:1-28 – You are precious to God.
Is 49:15-26 – God loves you like a mother loves her child.
Ws 3:1-9 – Those who love God receive His grace and mercy.
Ps 90:1-17 – God's love for frail man.
Ps 91:1-16 – You are secure under God's protection.
Ps 81:10-16 – God present among His Chosen People.
Mt 26:7-13 – Christ's love for the sinful woman.
Mt 18:12-14 – Christ's love for the Lost Sheep.
Jn 10:11-16 – Christ, the Good Shepherd.

Note: Quotations from the Holy Scriptures are taken from The Jerusalem Bible. Abbreviations referring to the books of the Bible are the abbreviations used in The Jerusalem Bible.

Lesson 2: THE GOD WHO LOVES YOU

1. God Teaches You About Himself

The God Who loves you manifests Himself to you in various ways to gain your love and to unite you to Himself forever. God teaches you through the things He has created; He also teaches you through Revelation.

2. God Teaches You He Exists

Through the marvelous world around you, God teaches you that He exists.

> Yes, naturally stupid are all men who have not known God and who, from the good things that are seen, have not been able to discover Him-Who-is, or, by studying the works, have failed to recognize the Artificer. Fire, however, or wind, or the swift air, the sphere of the stars, impetuous water, heaven's lamps, are what they have held to be the gods who govern the world. If, charmed by their beauty, they have taken things for gods, let them know how much the Lord of these excels them, since the very Author of beauty has created them. And if they have been impressed by their power and energy, let them deduce from these how much mightier is He that has formed them, since through the grandeur and beauty of the creatures we may, by analogy, contemplate the Author. Ws 13:1-5

The clouds in the sky, the flowers in the field, the little children at play, the massive mountains, the heat of the sun, the power of the freezing cold, the terror of the storm—all are made by God to teach you He exists.

3. God Comes To You Through Revelation

God so loves you that He is not satisfied to have you learn of Him only through the world He has created for you. He reveals Himself also through Revelation. Revelation is God making Himself known, His will, His Message of Salvation.

God gradually revealed Himself to the human race as a God of Salvation. He came first to the Jewish Community making clearer and clearer His existence and love for them in the Old Testament. Through Christ God revealed Himself completely in the New Testament.

Sacred Scripture is the Word of God placed in writing under the inspiration of the Holy Spirit. God is the Author of Sacred Scripture.

Sacred Tradition is the Word of God entrusted by Christ the Lord and the Holy Spirit to the apostles and handed on to their successors in its full purity. Second Vatican Council

> This Tradition which comes from the apostles develops in the Church with the help of the Holy Spirit. For there is a growth in the understanding of the realities and the words which have been handed down. This happens through the contemplation and study made by believers, who treasure these things in their hearts, through the intimate understanding of spiritual things they experience, and through the preaching of those who have received through episcopal succession the sure gift of truth. For, as the centuries succeed one another, the Church constantly moves forward toward the fullness of Divine truth until the Words of God reach their complete fulfillment in her. *Second Vatican Council*

Sacred Tradition and Sacred Scripture form one sacred deposit of the Word of God.

In revealing Himself through Sacred Scripture and Tradition God shows His consideration and love for you. God's Word is living and powerful. *The Word of God is something alive and active: it cuts like a double-edged sword but more finely: it can slip through the place where the soul is divided from the spirit, or joints from the marrow; it can judge the secret emotions and thoughts.* Heb 4:12. God's Word produces faith, devotion and reform in the hearts of those who will read it prayerfully.

4. God Is All-Holy

God is All-Holy because He is God. Isaiah the prophet tells us of the holiness of God: *I saw the Lord Yahweh seated on a high throne; His train filled the sanctuary; above Him stood seraphs, each one with six wings: two to cover its face, two to cover its feet and two for flying. And they cried out one to another in this way, "Holy, holy, holy is Yahweh Sabaoth. His glory fills the whole earth."* Is 6:1-3

God invites you and helps you to a life of holiness: *Be holy, for I, Yahweh your God, am holy.* Lv 19:2. His Son, Jesus

Christ, tells us how holy we should be: *You must therefore be perfect just as your heavenly Father is perfect.* Mt 5:48. This is the All-Holy God Who loves you so much.

5. God Is Goodness Itself

It is not necessary to demonstrate to you the goodness of God. From the depth of His love, God has given you all the good things you have. And He has no need of you whatsoever! King David in the Psalms speaks for you the joy that should be yours when you realize the goodness of God: *Give thanks to Yahweh, for He is good, His love is everlasting!* Ps 118:1-2. Again David says: *Praise Yahweh, for Yahweh is good. Play for His name, for He inspires love.* Ps 135:3

You should always remember that God can and often does bring good out of evil. St. Paul teaches us: *We know that by turning everything to their good, God cooperates with all those who love Him, with all those that He has called according to His purpose.* Rm 8:28. As you are being drawn closer to God be prepared to accept some suffering in your life. *This, in fact, is what you were called to do, because Christ suffered for you and left an example for you to follow the way He took. He was insulted and did not retaliate with insults; when He was tortured He made no threats but He put His trust in the righteous Judge.* 1 P 2:21-23

God permits some evil like illness, poverty, even sin to come into the lives of His loved ones in the world. God permits evil in the life of a person to punish a person for sin and to purify him from sin. Evil in a life frequently teaches a person to turn to God in prayer. Many have become like Jesus from poverty or illness.

6. God Is All-Powerful

The Book of Wisdom tells us of the mighty power of God: *For Your great strength is always at Your call; who can withstand the might of Your arm? In Your sight the whole world is like a grain of dust that tips the scales, like a drop of morning dew falling on the ground. Yet You are merciful to all, because You can do all things and overlook men's sins so that they can repent.* Ws 11:21-23

The power of God is manifested to us in the mammoth mountains, in the boundless seas or in the flash of lightning and the crack of the thunder of a storm. *Lord, You are great, You are glorious, wonderfully strong, unconquerable. May Your whole creation serve You! For You spoke and things came into being, You sent Your breath and they were put together, and no one can resist Your voice.* Jdt 16:16-17

You should have faith in God your loving Father and in His power. He will do everything necessary to give you a happy life here and in heaven forever, if you will give yourself to Him. *For nothing is impossible to God.* Lk 1:37

7. God Is Present Everywhere

A great consolation in life is the knowledge that God is everywhere. Because He is a loving Father, He is always present wherever you go to help you and to console you, even to chide you if you have committed sin. David says it so well: *Where could I go to escape Your spirit? Where could I flee from Your presence? If I climb the heavens, You are there, there too, if I lie in Sheol. If I flew to the point of sunrise, or westward across the sea, Your hand would still be guiding me, Your right hand holding me.* Ps 139:7-10

8. God Knows Everything

God knows even your most secret thoughts, words and actions. *He has fathomed the deep and the heart, and seen into their devious ways; for the Most High knows all the knowledge there is, and has observed the signs of the times. He declares what is past and what will be, and uncovers the traces of hidden things. Not a thought escapes Him, not a single word is hidden from Him.* Si 42:18-20. In the New Testament Paul reminds us of the same truth:

> No created thing can hide from Him; everything is uncovered and open to the eyes of the One to Whom we must give account of ourselves. Heb 4:13

9. God Is Truthful And Faithful To His Promises

God can neither deceive nor be deceived. *God is no man that He should lie, no Son of Adam to draw back. Is it His to say and not to do, to speak and not fulfill?* Nb 23:19. He promises you love, happiness and peace and will give these great gifts to you if you have faith in Him and turn to Him.

By revealing Himself to you as your All-Holy God, Goodness-Itself, Powerful, Present Everywhere, All-Knowing and All-Truthful, the God of Salvation tries to lead you to union with Himself. *The heavens declare the glory of God, the vault of heaven proclaims His handiwork.* Ps 19:1. The Book of Job teaches: *If you would learn more, ask the cattle, seek information from the birds of the air. The creeping things of earth will give you lessons, and the fishes of the sea will tell you all. . . . He holds in His power the soul of every living thing, and the breath of each man's body.* Jb 12:7-10

10. There Are Three Persons In God

In Revelation God has manifested to us that there are three Persons in the Godhead, God the Father, God the Son and God the Holy Spirit. In His mandate to baptize Jesus tells of the three Persons: *Go, therefore, make disciples of all the nations; baptize them in the name of the Father and of the Son and of the Holy Spirit.* Mt 28: 19-20

CHRISTIAN PRACTICE

Walk alone under the sky, admire God's creation, be drawn to prayer and union with God.

Try to enter into the sentiments of David in Psalm 29 as he realized the holiness, goodness, power and providence of God: *Pay tribute to Yahweh, you sons of God, tribute to Yahweh of glory and power, tribute to Yahweh of the glory of His name, worship Yahweh in His sacred court. The voice of Yahweh over the waters! Yahweh over the multitudinous waters! The voice of Yahweh in power! The voice of Yahweh in splendor! The voice of Yahweh shatters the cedars, Yahweh shatters the cedars of Lebanon, making Lebanon leap like a calf, Sirion like a young wild bull. The voice of Yahweh sharpens lightning shafts! The voice of Yahweh sets the wilderness shaking. Yahweh shakes the wilderness of Kadesh. The voice of Yahweh sets the terebinths shuddering, stripping the forests bare. The God of glory thunders. In His palace everything cries 'Glory!' Yahweh sat enthroned for the Flood, Yahweh sits enthroned as a King for ever. Yahweh gives strength to His people, Yahweh blesses His people with peace.*

CHRISTIAN PRAYER

Holy, Holy, Holy Lord, God of power and might, heaven and earth are full of Your glory. Hosanna in the highest. Blessed is He Who comes in the name of the Lord. Hosanna in the highest. *The Mass*

Sing Yahweh a new song! Sing to Yahweh, all the earth! Sing to Yahweh, bless His name. Proclaim His Salvation day after day, tell of His glory among the nations, tell His marvels to every people. Yahweh is great, loud must be His praise, He is to be feared beyond all gods. Nothingness, all the gods of the nations. Yahweh Himself made the heavens, in His presence are splendor and majesty, in His sanctuary power and beauty. Pay tribute to Yahweh, families of the peoples, tribute to Yahweh of glory and power, tribute to Yahweh of His name's due glory. Bring out the offering, bear it before Him, worship Yahweh in His sacred court, tremble before Him, all the earth! Say among the nations, Yahweh is King! Firm has He made the world, and unshakeable; He will judge each nation with strict justice. Let the heavens be glad, let earth rejoice, let the sea thunder and all that it holds, let the fields exult and all that is in them, let all the woodland trees cry out for joy, at the presence of Yahweh, for He comes, He comes to judge the earth, to judge the world with justice and the nations with His truth. Ps 96

God of our ancestors, Lord of Mercy, Who by Your word have made all things, and in Your wisdom have fitted man to rule the creatures that have come from You, to govern the world in holiness and justice and in honesty of soul to wield authority, grant me wisdom, consort of Your throne, and do not reject me from the number of Your children. For I am Your servant, son of Your serving maid, a feeble man, with little time to live, with small understanding of justice and the laws. Ws 9:1-5

SUGGESTED READING FROM SCRIPTURE

In His goodness and wisdom, God chose to reveal Himself and to make known to us the hidden purpose of His will. *Second Vatican Council*

Jr 23:23-24 – God is everywhere.
Ps 71:1-24 – The Majesty of God.
Ps 103:1-22; 104:1-35; 105:1-11 – The Majesty of God.
Ex 19:1-25; 20:1-21 – The Majesty of God shown in His giving the Israelites the commandments.
1 Jn 1:5-7 – God is Light.
Nb 23:19 – God is truthful.
Jn 8:31-59 – Jesus teaches truth.
Jn 18:33-38 – Christ the King came to give testimony to the truth.
Rv 1-1-8 – God our beginning and end.

Lesson 3: GOD CREATED THE HEAVEN AND THE EARTH AND ALL THINGS

1. God Created The Earth

God created the earth.

> Thus heaven and earth were completed with all their array. On the seventh day God completed the work He had been doing. He rested on the seventh day after all the work He had been doing. God blessed the seventh day and made it holy, because on that day He had rested after all His work of creating. Such were the origins of heaven and earth when they were created. At the time when Yahweh God made earth and heaven there was as yet no wild bush on the earth nor had any wild plant yet sprung up, for Yahweh God had not sent rain on the earth, nor was there any man to till the soil. Gn 2:1-5

God created the earth and all the good things in it because He wanted to share with you His riches. He shares His riches with you because of His boundless love for you.

2. God Created Man

Against the false concepts of man they had learned in Eastern myths, the Hebrews gave us the true concept of man and the special favor shown him by God. Hebrew Scriptures tell us that God created as special beings far above all the rest of creation a man and a woman. We have called this man and this woman Adam and Eve. *Yahweh God fashioned man of dust from the soil. Then He breathed into his nostrils a breath of life and, thus man became a living being.* Gn 2:7

God made man in His own image: *God said, "Let Us make man in Our own image, in the likeness of Ourselves."* Gn 1:26. Because you are a person you are like God; you can think, reflect, analyze and do creative things. You have intelligence, understanding and free will; you can choose to do one thing or another; you can choose good or evil. Your soul is immortal; it will never die as long as God exists so will your soul live on.

You should realize your dignity as a man and thank God, your Father, who gave you such dignity. *Ah, what is man that You should spare a thought for him, the son of man that You should care for him? Yet You have made him little less than a god, You have crowned him with glory and splendor.* Ps 8:4-5. Because you are a man you are a wonderful and mysterious combination of matter and spirit, body and soul. A man is a little world of God's creation having in himself all the parts of the world God made. Like a plant a man eats food and grows. Like an animal he has senses and animal appetites. Like God and the angels he has a spiritual part, his soul.

You must show reverence to yourself and to every man because each man has the high dignity of being created in the likeness of God. You must respect all people of other races and religions. You must respect even your enemies because they too are dignified people created by God.

3. God Created Man For Himself

Man is from God—therefore he is for God. You were not made just to eat, sleep, work, marry, and grow old. You were not made by God to search continually for pleasure, entertainment, money, fame. You were placed in this world to know and love God and be happy with Him forever in the next world. You were made for God. You will live forever with God in heaven if you will love Him now.

4. Angels

Angels in the Scripture and in our Catholic liturgy impress the Christian with the majesty of God.

> I saw the Lord Yahweh seated on a high throne; His train filled the sanctuary; above Him stood seraphs, each one with six wings: two to cover its face, two to cover its feet and two for flying. And they cried out one to another in this way, "Holy, holy, holy is Yahweh Sabaoth. His glory fills the whole earth." Is 6:1-3

In the Catholic liturgy at Mass we frequently say or sing:

> And so, with all the choirs of angels in heaven we proclaim Your glory and join in their unending hymn of praise: Holy, Holy, Holy Lord, God of power and might, heaven and earth are full of Your glory, Hosanna in the highest. Blessed is He Who comes in the name of the Lord. Hosanna in the highest.

Every man's struggle with evil is graphically portrayed in the Scripture as a fight against an evil person: *For it is not against human enemies that we have to struggle, but against the Sovereignties and the Powers who originate the darkness in this world, the spiritual army of evil in the heavens.* Ep 6:12

CHRISTIAN PRACTICE

Give God thanks every day for creating you.

Treat yourself and every man with reverence because God has created all men.

Make your home a more pleasant one.

Practice being polite to others.

Because of your dignity as a human being be careful of your language.

Remember that other persons deserve your respect, so be patient if they cause you pain.

Try to make your neighborhood a Christian community by the way you act.

Christian parents should realize from this lesson that their children are God-like beings whom they are to lead to a love of God.

CHRISTIAN PRAYER

Our Father, Who art in heaven, hallowed by Thy name; Thy kingdom come; Thy will be done on earth as it is in heaven. Give us this day our daily bread; and forgive us our trespasses as we forgive those who trespass against us, and lead us not into temptation, but deliver us from evil.

O God, Creator of all things, despise not those who have sinned against You; rather, give us the grace of repentance that we may be sharers in the new Creation.

SUGGESTED READING FROM SCRIPTURE

God, Who through the Word creates all things and keeps them in existence, gives men an enduring witness to Himself in created realities.
Second Vatican Council

Gn 1:24:31; 2:18-20 – God created the animals, man and then He rested.
Pr 22:1-29 – All men are equal in the sight of God.
Tb 8:7 – The works of Creation lead us to God.
Dn 3:57-90 – The works of Creation lead man to adore God.
Ps 148:1-14; 149:1-3 – God's world praises Him.
Jb 12:7-10 – Creation tells us of God.
Ps 18:2-5 – The heaven shows the glory of God.
Ws 13:1-5 – All men know something of God through His Creation.

Lesson 4: GOD GIVES YOU HIS DIVINE LIFE

1. Grace Is A New Life Of The Soul, A Sharing In The Life Of God Himself

Grace is God's gift of Himself: *If anyone loves Me he will keep My word, and My Father will love him, and We shall come to him and make Our home with him.* Jn 14:23. From God's gift of Himself comes our life in God which is the life of grace.

> In making these gifts, He has given us the guarantee of something very great and wonderful to come: through them you will be able to share the Divine nature and to escape corruption in a world that is sunk in vice. But to attain this, you will have to do your utmost yourselves, adding goodness to the faith that you have, understanding to your goodness, self-control to your understanding, patience to your self-control, true devotion to your patience, kindness towards your fellow men to your devotion, and, to this kindness, love. 2 P 1:4-7

2. Grace Is The Most Startling Fact Of God's Love For You

Grace makes the soul so beautiful that the soul becomes like God and so delights God that it is most dearly loved by Him. It is adopted as His child and spouse and is elevated from earth to heaven. By grace the soul is received into the bosom of the Eternal Father; and with Jesus Christ, the Divine Son, that soul participates in the very nature of God even while on this earth. St. Thomas teaches that the whole world itself and all the world contains is of far less value before God than the grace in a single soul. St. Augustine maintains that heaven, together with all the angels, cannot be compared to God's grace in a human soul.

3. Through Grace God Gives You A Participation In His Life

A person gets two lives from God. One is the natural life he obtains at birth. The other is the second he receives when he is baptized a Christian. *I tell you most solemnly, unless a man is born from above, he cannot see the kingdom of God.* Jn 3:3

4. Through Grace You Become A Son Of God

You obtain natural life from your father and mother; you

obtain supernatural life from God, your Father. You are like God your Father because you have His life! You become God-like. St. John makes it clear: *Think of the love that the Father has lavished on us, by letting us be called God's children; and that is what we are.* 1 Jn 3:1. Christians are sons of God: *Everyone moved by the Spirit is a son of God. The spirit you received is not the spirit of slaves bringing fear into your lives again; it is the spirit of sons, and it makes us cry out, "Abba, Father!" The Spirit Himself and our spirit bear united witness that we are children of God. And if we are children we are heirs as well: heirs of God and coheirs with Christ, sharing His sufferings so as to share His glory.* Rm 8:14-17. Christians are God's children: *By His own choice He made us His children by the message of the truth so that we should be a sort of first-fruits of all that He had created.* Jm 1:18

5. Through Grace God Lives In You

God lives in you when you have His grace. *If anyone loves Me he will keep My word, and My Father will love him, and We shall come to him and make Our home with him.* Jn 14:23. Christians are temples of God: *Didn't you realize that you were God's temple and that the Spirit of God was living among you?* 1 Co 3:16

6. God Gave His Grace To Adam And Eve

God gave His grace to Adam and Eve. Grace was the greatest of God's gifts to the first man and woman. Through grace Adam and Eve shared in the very life of God; Adam and Eve actually were sons of God; God lived in them as He lives in a temple.

7. By Their Sin Adam And Eve Lost God's Life

Through some great catastrophe the human race lost God's life, grace. St. Paul narrates the fact in language made clear for all: *Well then, sin entered the world through one man, and through sin death, and thus death has spread through the whole human race because everyone has sinned. . . . Yet death reigned over all from Adam to Moses.* Rm 5:12-14. We place the name Original Sin on the catastrophe of man losing his God.

The temptation and fall of our first parents are recorded in the first book of the Bible:

> The serpent was the most subtle of all the wild beasts that Yahweh God had made. It asked the woman, "Did God really say you were not to eat from any of the trees in the garden?" The woman answered the serpent, "We may eat the fruit of the trees in the garden. But of the fruit of the tree in the middle of the garden God said, 'You must not eat it, nor touch it, under pain of death.'" Then the serpent said to the woman, "No! You will not die! God knows in fact that on the day you eat it your eyes will be opened and you will be like gods, knowing good and evil." The woman saw that the tree was good to eat and pleasing to the eye, and that it was desirable for the knowledge that it could give. So she took some of its fruit and ate it. She gave some also to her husband who was with her, and he ate it. Gn 3:1-7

8. God Regained Grace For You And For All Men And Showed Us What It Means To Be Sons Of God

Because of His love for us Jesus regained grace for all men and showed us what it means to be sons of God. *Yes, God loved the world so much that He gave His only Son, so that everyone who believes in Him may not be lost but may have eternal life.* Jn 3:16

> If it is certain that through one man's fall so many died, it is even more certain that Divine grace, coming through the one man, Jesus Christ, came to so many as an abundant free gift. The results of the gift also outweigh the result of one man's sin: for after one single fall came judgment with a verdict of condemnation, now after many falls comes grace with its verdict of acquittal. If it is certain that death reigned over everyone as the consequence of one man's fall, it is even more certain that one man, Jesus Christ, will cause everyone to reign in life who receives the free gift that he does not deserve, of being made righteous. Again, as one man's fall brought condemnation on everyone, so the good act of one man brings everyone life and makes them justified. As by one man's disobedience many were made sinners, so by one man's obedience many will be made righteous. Rm 5:15-19

The joy of Christ which the Christian soul experiences comes from the sin of Adam: *O necessary sin of Adam, which was blotted out by the death of Christ. O happy fault, that merited such a Redeemer.* Easter Vigil

9. You Should Yearn For God's Life

You should yearn for God's life. To receive God's life you must accept Jesus, His way of life and His baptism. *"You must repent," Peter answered "and every one of you must be baptized in the name of Jesus Christ for the forgiveness of your sins, and you will receive the gift of the Holy Spirit. The promise that was made is for you and your children, and for all those who are far away, for all those whom the Lord our God will call to Himself."* Ac 2:38-39. The clear teaching of St. Paul impresses us: *You have been taught that when we were baptized in Christ Jesus we were baptized in His death; in other words, when we were baptized we went into the tomb with Him and joined Him in death, so that as Christ was raised from the dead by the Father's glory, we too might live a new life.* Rm 6:3-4

10. After Your Commitment to Christ You Ought To Live As A Christian

By serious sin you can lose God's life regained for you by your Redeemer Christ. Serious sin is the rebellion of an ungrateful son against God His Father. *Is this the return you make to Yahweh? O foolish, unwise people!* Dt 32:6. Serious sin makes you unhappy and sometimes even a slave to sin. *I tell you most solemnly, everyone who commits sin is a slave. Now the slave's place in the house is not assured, but the son's place is assured. So if the Son makes you free, you will be free indeed.* Jn 8:34-36. A serious violation of the law of God is called a serious sin, a deadly sin, a mortal sin because it destroys God's life, grace, in the human soul. A less serious sin, a small violation of the law of God, is called a venial sin and does not deprive the soul of God's life, but of course should be avoided.

11. The Committed Christian Should Avoid The Evil Things In The World

The evil persons, places, and things in this world can lead even the committed Christian into sin. *You must not love this passing world or anything that is in the world, because nothing the world has to offer—the sensual body, the lustful eye, pride in possessions—could ever come from the Father but only from the world; and the world, with all it craves for, is coming to an end; but anyone who does the will of God remains for ever.* 1 Jn 2:15-17

The inclinations of your body tempt you to do things unworthy of a Christian. *For a perishable body presses down the soul.* Ws 9:15. Every man experiences in himself tendencies to sin. These tendencies are lust, laziness, gluttony, anger, greed, envy, pride and neglect of the needs of one's neighbor.

> For it is not against human enemies that we have to struggle, but against the sovereignties and the powers who originate the darkness in this world, the spiritual army of evil in the heavens. That is why you must rely on God's armor, or you will not be able to put up any resistance when the worst happens, or have enough resources to hold your ground. So stand your ground, with truth buckled around your waist, and integrity for a breastplate, wearing for shoes on your feet the eagerness to spread the gospel of peace and always carrying the shield of faith so that you can use it to put out the burning arrows of the evil one. Ep 6:11-16

In the Ephesians just quoted the power of evil in the world tempting all to sin is explained by St. Paul.

12. Realize Your Dignity, Christian

From a realization of your Christian worth and dignity you will set goals for your life and train yourself to keep God's grace as your most precious possession. The sacrifice necessary to stay away from sin and the practice of love of God and other men is the way to maintain your dignity. You can now say prayerfully the Psalm of David: *Ah, what is man that You should spare a thought for him, the son of man that You should care for him? Yet You have made him little less than a god, You have crowned him with glory and splendor, made him lord over the work of Your hands, set all things under his feet, sheep and oxen, all these, yes, wild animals too, birds in the air, fish in the sea traveling the paths of the ocean.* Ps 8:4-8

CHRISTIAN PRACTICE

Sit or kneel before a crucifix. See how God loved you so much that He restored grace to you by having His Son die for you.

In your daily life remember St. Paul's exhortation: *Didn't you realize that you were God's temple and that the Spirit of God was living among you?* 1 Co 3:16

Since the Spirit is our life, let us be directed by the Spirit. Ga 5:25

When you make the sign of the cross remember that you are telling everyone that you belong to God.

If anyone loves Me he will keep My word, and My Father will love him, and We shall come to him and make Our home with him. Jn 14:23

CHRISTIAN PRAYER

It is proper and just that with all the ardor of our hearts and minds we should proclaim with our voices the Almighty Father and His Only-begotten Son, Our Lord Jesus Christ, Who paid the debt of Adam for us to His Eternal Father, and with His precious blood washed away the penalty of Original Sin. This is the paschal feast in which the true Lamb is slain; Whose Blood hallowed the door-posts of the faithful. This is the night on which You brought our forefathers, the children of Israel, dry-shod through the Red Sea in the flight from Egypt. This is the night on which the light of the pillar of fire destroyed the darkness of sin. This is the night which at this hour everywhere restores to grace and unites in holiness those who believe in Christ, separating them from worldly vice and the darkness of sin. This is the night on which Christ burst the bonds of death and victoriously arose from the grave. For life itself, without Redemption, would be of no avail to us. O wondrous condescension of Your mercy towards us! How far beyond our understanding is Your loving affection, that You should ransom a slave at the price of Your Son. O necessary sin of Adam, which was erased out by the death of Christ. O happy fault, that merited such a Redeemer. O truly blessed night which alone deserved to know the time and the hour when Christ arose from the grave. *Easter Vigil*

SUGGESTED READING FROM SCRIPTURE

Through Divine Revelation, God chose to show forth and communicate Himself and the eternal decisions of His will regarding the Salvation of men. That is to say, He chose to share those Divine treasures which totally transcend the understanding of the human mind. *Second Vatican Council*

Jn 3:1-17 – Jesus tells Nicodemus of the Christian rebirth.
Jn 15:1-8 – Christians get life from Christ the Vine.
Rm 5:12-19 – Salvation comes through faith and grace.
Ep 2:1-10 – You are saved by grace through faith.
2 P 1:4-8 – God has called us to share His Divine nature.
Gn 3:1-19 – The parents of the whole human race fell into sin.

Gn 6:11-23 – God destroyed the whole world with a flood because of sin, saving only Noah and his family.
Gn 9:8-17 – God promised that He would never again destroy the world with a flood.

Jesus Christ
The Son Of God

Lesson 5: THE GOD OF SALVATION PREPARES US FOR THE COMING OF HIS SON, JESUS CHRIST

1. Introduction

The first four lessons in this book teach us the love of God for you: what God has revealed about Himself, God's creation for love of you and God's desire to give you His Divine life. God gives His Divine life through Jesus.

In chapters five to ten we shall see who Jesus is, why He came and what He did. To understand Jesus better, we shall briefly look at key events in The History of Salvation which happened before Jesus was born. In this way, we shall better appreciate how God prepared mankind for the birth of Jesus.

In this way too, we can understand God's wonderful Message of Salvation for all of us, His mercy, His love.

2. The History Of Salvation — Time Chart

God creates man	The dawn of human history
God calls Abraham	1850 B.C.
God delivers His people from Egypt	1240 B.C.
The Sinai Covenant	1220 B.C.
The Israelites in the Promised Land await the Savior	1200 B.C.
The United Kingdom of the Jews	1000 B.C.
The Northern Kingdom, Israel, falls— the Assyrian Captivity	721 B.C.
The Southern Kingdom falls— the Babylonian captivity	587 B.C.
The Judeans return from captivity	538 B.C.
The Birth of Jesus	4 B.C.

3. God Creates Man

Man, the human race, graphically described with names

Adam and Eve, was the high point of God's creation. To man God gave the gift of grace, God's life.

All of this would have been ours as descendants of Adam and Eve. But a tragedy took place which changed the life of mankind. This tragic event is called the Original Sin.

4. Adam And Eve: The Original Sin

Adam and Eve were created in grace, sharing God's life. God also created them to be free creatures. Through their free obedience to God, they would begin human history in a successful way for themselves and us.

God required of our first parents that they would recognize Him as their Father and give Him fitting love, service and obedience. God gave Adam and Eve a strict command. This command was so important that if Adam and Eve had obeyed God, all their gifts would have been ours too.

Adam and Eve, however, chose not to obey God. They proudly chose to be self-reliant. They rejected God's fatherly friendship. This rebellion is called Original Sin.

Adam and Eve committed this sin themselves, but they were not the only ones to suffer the consequences. We are affected by the Original Sin. We are born in a situation of being apart from God and His friendship. We begin our human lives without a share in God's life. We are subject to pain, sickness and hardships of every kind. We are lonely in a world filled with other people. We are all too ready to show selfishness and pride. Wars are so much a part of our lives that we almost take them for granted. God gives us freedom, but it is very difficult for us not to repeat over and over again the disobedience of our first parents. We are prone to sinning.

This is our lot in life as children of Adam and Eve, even though we are not personally guilty of the Original Sin. To understand ourselves and what Jesus did to save us, we have to believe in this early tragedy, which happened through the free choice of Adam and Eve.

5. God Calls Abraham

God began to prepare for Jesus to be born of a particular race of people by calling Abraham in the year about 1850 B.C. Abraham lived in Ur near the Persian Gulf.

Why God chose Abraham, and not someone else, was God's will. The importance of Abraham lies in the promise God made to him: *Leave your country, your family and your father's house, for the land I will show you. I will make you a great nation; I will bless you and make your name so famous that it will be used as a blessing. I will bless those who bless you: I will curse those who slight you. All the tribes of the earth shall bless themselves by you.* Gn 12:1-3

And so God promised that Abraham would become the father of a great nation, that a land would be theirs, and that all nations would be blessed through Abraham. This was certainly not a clear-cut promise of an individual Savior.

Abraham obeyed God. He took everything with him as he left his native land setting out for an unknown destination. Abraham gave himself entirely in self-surrender to God's will, without knowing what the future would hold. God promised Abraham that he would be the father of a great people, and yet Abraham was already an old man. Abraham accepted God's Word with faith and lived out his response to God. This dynamic faith of Abraham merits for him the title of Father of Faith.

God made a covenant or agreement with Abraham. He would be their God if they would be His people. The two main points to remember about Abraham are: 1) He was Father of the Chosen People; 2) He was Father of the faithful which means that Abraham fathered a people who needed faith like his own to realize their great destiny.

Later, the descendants of Abraham would renew for themselves God's covenant with Abraham. They would worship together and recall: *My father was a wandering Aramean.* Dt 26:5

6. God Delivers His People From Egypt

During the next 600 years, Abraham's family grew into a loosely-knit people. The Chosen People, made up of twelve tribes, were now called Israelites. We find the Israelites in Egypt, where they had lived for many generations. How or why they originally came to Egypt is not very important. The way in which they finally left Egypt is of great importance.

At first, the Israelites found Egypt to be a pleasant place. Then around 1300 B.C., an Egyptian Pharaoh, unfriendly toward the Israelites, came into power. He humiliated them with slavery and forced them to build a city. Forced slavery was hard to bear for the Israelites. But another kind of slavery, brought on by the Israelites themselves, was even more oppressive. They had forgotten about the God of their father, Abraham. So they lost sight of their special destiny as God's Chosen People. The Israelites were slaves to their own sins. Nevertheless, God kept true to His Promise. He remained faithful to the covenant made with Abraham.

From among the Israelites, God selected Moses as leader. Through Moses, God would deliver His own people from slavery in Egypt. God told Moses: *I am the God of your father, . . . And now the cry of the sons of Israel has come to Me, and I have witnessed the way in which the Egyptians oppress them, so come, I send you to Pharaoh to bring the sons of Israel, My people, out of Egypt.* Ex 3:6-10. Moses hesitated, but did as God told him.

After many confrontations with Moses, Pharoah finally agreed to release the slaves. The weary Israelites, led by Moses, started on their way. Soon Pharoah changed his mind. He ordered his army, the best in the world, to track down the Israelites and force them back into slavery. The Israelites thought God had betrayed them. Moses gave encouragement to his people.

In a surprising turn of events, the highly trained Egyptians were defeated and killed in a sea of reeds. The Israelites, however, passed successfully through the marsh and were saved. The Chosen People believed that God alone deserved credit for their narrow escape: *Israel witnessed the great act that Yahweh had performed against the Egyptians, and the people venerated Yahweh; they put their faith in Yahweh and in Moses, His servant.* Ex 14:31

7. The Sinai Covenant

God continued to care for His people as they marched through the desert. Strangely enough, the Israelites did not appreciate God's love for them. They often murmured their discontent to Moses.

At Mount Sinai, in the Arabian Desert, God made another covenant with His people. God first reminded Moses of how the Israelites had been miraculously delivered from Egypt. Then God promised that He would continue to care for the ungrateful Israelites. They, in turn, would live as God's people by obeying the Ten Commandments which God now gave to Moses. God's words strikingly sum up this new covenant at Sinai: *I am your God, and you are My People.* The Chosen People were to show their love for God by obeying the Ten Commandments. In this way, they would show their gratitude to God for everything He had done for them.

The Chosen People also shared a sacred meal together. Thus they expressed their brotherhood. The covenant, the living bond between God and the Israelites, would mean nothing unless real brotherhood existed among the Israelites themselves.

God's deliverance of the Israelites from Egypt and the Sinai Covenant were the big event in Salvation History before the coming of Jesus Christ. Since the Israelites were supposed to remain aware of their covenant relationship with God, God ordered the Sinai Covenant to be celebrated and renewed often. This did not happen. The Israelites quickly forgot that God had delivered them. They repeatedly violated God's commandments and thereby broke the covenant. Nevertheless, their faith in God was the prevailing characteristic of the Chosen People as they made their way toward the Promised Land.

8. The Israelites In The Promised Land Await The Savior

Around 1200 B.C., the Israelites crossed the Jordan River into the land once promised to Abraham. Strong opposition met the newcomers. With God on their side, the Israelites succeeded in capturing most of the Promised Land. The territory was then divided among the twelve tribes of Israel. There was no overall unity among the Israelites.

9. The United Kingdom Of The Jews

About the year 1000 B.C., all twelve tribes were united in

one kingdom. David and his son, Solomon, were the most famous kings.

10. The Kingdom Is Divided

The glory and power of a united nation lasted only seventy years. Both political and religious unity was lost as the kingdom divided in two: Israel—Northern tribes and Judea—Southern tribes.

11. The Northern Kingdom Falls—The Assyrian Captivity

Some 200 years later, Israel, the Northern kingdom, fell at the hands of the Assyrians. The victors took their captives back to Assyria. When the exiled people returned to their homeland, they married with people of other nationalities. This custom disgusted the Judeans, the people of the South. The Judeans felt that the Northern tribes had betrayed God. God's Chosen People should not marry unbelievers. The two kingdoms, Israel and Judea, remained divided.

12. The Southern Kingdom Falls—The Babylonian Captivity

The Kingdom of Judea kept its independence for 250 more years. Finally, in 587 B.C., the Babylonians overran Judea, and exiled the Judeans to Babylonia.

13. The Judeans Return From Captivity

Fifty years later, the Persians conquered the Babylonians. The Hebrews returned to Judea. In 333 B.C., the Greeks defeated the Persians and controlled Palestine. Around 60 B.C., the Roman Empire spread into the Middle East and controlled Palestine.

14. The Birth Of Jesus

During the reign of Caesar Augustus, the Roman Emperor, Jesus Christ the Son of God was born in Bethlehem of Judea.

CHRISTIAN PRACTICE

Read a few pages of the Old Testament each day so that you can appreciate the way God prepared mankind for our Savior Jesus Christ.

CHRISTIAN PRAYER

We beseech You, Almighty God, grant us an awareness of our weakness, so that we may place our trust in Your strength and rejoice forever in Your fatherly love. Amen. *Mass of the Fourth Week of Lent*

O God, we behold Your ancient wonders shining even to our own time; for that which the power of Your right hand did for one people, in freeing them from Egyptian bondage, You accomplished now for the Salvation of all men by the waters of re-birth. Grant that the whole world may become children of Abraham and enter into the heritage of Israel. Through our Lord Jesus Christ, Your Son, Who is living and reigning with You in the unity of the Holy Spirit, one God, for ever and ever. *Amen.*

O God, by the voice of Your prophets You have made known to all the children of Your Church that You Yourself are the sower of good seed and the Husbandman of the chosen vine in every field of Your domain. You have made this present people Your vineyard and Your harvest. Grant them, therefore, Your strength to root out the tangle of briars and thorns, and to bring forth worthy fruit in abundance. Through our Lord Jesus Christ, Your Son, Who is living and reigning with You in the unity of the Holy Spirit, one God, for ever and ever. *Amen.*

SUGGESTED READING FROM SCRIPTURE

In carefully planning and preparing the Salvation of the whole human race, the God of supreme love, by a special dispensation, chose for Himself a people to whom He might entrust His promises. *Second Vatican Council*

> Although a reading of the entire Old Testament is a good way to know, understand and appreciate The History of Salvation, the student at this point should be directed to find a suitable guide for his initial study of Salvation History. "Reading the Word of God" by Lawrence Dannemiller, S.S., Helicon Press, 1120 N. Calvert St., Baltimore, Maryland is suggested. Also suggested is "A Guide to Reading the Old Testament," Acta Publications, Chicago.

Lesson 6: JESUS CHRIST, THE SON OF GOD, OUR REDEEMER

1. The Redeemer

Who would redeem us from our sins? Who would regain for us the treasures of God's grace? In His promise to Adam and Eve after their fall into sin, God revealed to the human race the fact that He would send us a Redeemer: *I will make you enemies of each other: you and the woman, your offspring and her offspring. It will crush your head and you will strike its heel.* Gn 3:15. Who would teach us God's teaching in a world that neglects to learn of Him? God's Son, Jesus Christ our Lord and Savior. *But when the appointed time came, God sent His Son, born of a woman, born of a subject of the Law, to redeem the subjects of the Law and to enable us to be adopted as sons.* Ga 4:4-5. We rejoice with St. Paul:

> Blessed be God the Father of our Lord Jesus Christ, Who has blessed us with all the spiritual blessings of heaven in Christ. Before the world was made, He chose us, chose us in Christ, to be holy and spotless, and to live through love in His presence, determining that we should become His adopted sons, through Jesus Christ for His own kind purposes, to make us praise the glory of His grace, His free gift to us in the Beloved, in Whom, through His Blood, we gain our freedom, the forgiveness of our sins. Such is the richness of the grace which He has showered on us in all wisdom and insight. He has let us know the mystery of His purpose, the hidden plan He so kindly made in Christ from the beginning to act upon when the times had run their course to the end: that He would bring everything together under Christ, as head. Ep 1:3-10

2. The Angel Announces To Mary That She Is To Be The Mother Of Jesus

In the plan of our loving Father, His Son was to come to this world born of a woman.

> In the sixth month the angel Gabriel was sent by God to a town in Galilee called Nazareth, to a virgin betrothed to a man named Joseph, of the House of David; and the virgin's name was Mary. He went in and said to her, "Rejoice, so highly favored! The Lord is with you." She was deeply disturbed by these words and asked herself what this greeting could mean, but the angel said to her, "Mary, do not be afraid; you have won God's favor. Listen! You are to conceive and bear a son, and you must name Him Jesus. He will be great and will

be called Son of the Most High. The Lord God will give Him the throne of His ancestor David; He will rule over the House of Jacob for ever and His reign will have no end." Mary said to the angel, "But how can this come about, since I am a virgin?" "The Holy Spirit will come upon you" the angel answered "and the power of the Most High will cover you with its shadow. And so the child will be holy and will be called Son of God." Lk 1:26-36

St. Paul tells of the lowliness of Christ in becoming man:

In your minds you must be the same as Christ Jesus: His state was Divine, yet He did not cling to His equality with God but emptied Himself to assume the condition of a slave, and became as men are; and being as all men are, He was humbler yet, even to accepting death, death on a cross. But God raised Him high and gave Him the name which is above all other names so that all beings in the heavens, on earth and in the underworld, should bend the knee at the name of Jesus and that every tongue should acclaim Jesus Christ as Lord, to the glory of God the Father. Ph 2:5-11

3. Christ Was Born For Us

The story of Christmas is told by St. Luke:

And everyone went to his own town to be registered. So Joseph set out from the town of Nazareth in Galilee and traveled up to Judea, to the town of David called Bethlehem, since he was of David's House and line, in order to be registered together with Mary, his betrothed, who was with child. While they were there the time came for her to have her child, and she gave birth to a Son, her first-born. She wrapped Him in swaddling clothes, and laid Him in a manger because there was no room for them at the inn. In the countryside close by there were shepherds who lived in the fields and took it in turns to watch their flocks during the night. The angel of the Lord appeared to them and the glory of the Lord shone round them. They were terrified, but the angel said, "Do not be afraid. Listen, I bring you news of great joy, a joy to be shared by the whole people. Today in the town of David a Savior has been born to you; He is Christ the Lord. And here is a sign for you: you will find a baby wrapped in swaddling clothes and lying in a manger." And suddenly with the angel there was a great throng of the heavenly host, praising God and singing: "Glory to God in the highest heaven, and peace to men who enjoy His favor." Lk 2:3-14

In these most simple terms St. Luke made known to us the birth of God made man. To inspire us more and to lift our souls to recognize the tremendous reality, St. Paul tells us:

> You see, God's grace has been revealed, and it has made Salvation possible for the whole human race and taught us that what we have to do is to give up everything that does not lead to God, and all our wordly ambitions; we must be self-restrained and live good and religious lives here in this present world, while we are waiting in hope for the blessing which will come with the appearing of the glory of our great God and Savior Christ Jesus. He sacrificed Himself for us in order to set us free from all wickedness and to purify a people so that it could be His very own and would have no ambition except to do good. Tt 2:11-14

The joy and thanksgiving of the Christmas angels should be ours as we realize this tremendous mystery. At Midnight Mass on Christmas we pray:

> Father, All-powerful and Ever-living God, we do well always and everywhere to give You thanks through Jesus Christ our Lord. In the wonder of the incarnation Your Eternal Word has brought to the eyes of faith a new and radiant vision of Your glory. In Him we see our God made visible and so are caught up on love of the God we cannot see. And so, with all the choirs of angels in heaven we proclaim Your glory and join in their unending hymn of praise.

The prophecies of the Old Testament especially those of Isaiah help us to lift our hearts to the reality of Christmas: *The Lord Himself, therefore, will give you a sign. It is this: the maiden is with child and will soon give to a Son Whom she will call Immanuel.* Is 7:14. *For there is a child born to us, a Son given to us and dominion is laid on His shoulders; and this is the name they give Him: Wonder-Counsellor, Mighty-God, Eternal-Father, Prince-of-Peace.* Is 9:5-6. *The spirit of the Lord Yahweh has been given to me, for Yahweh has anointed me. He has sent me to bring good news to the poor, to bind up hearts that are broken; to proclaim liberty to captives, freedom to those in prison; to proclaim a year of favor from Yahweh, a day of vengeance for our God.* Is 61:1-2. *Courage! Do not be afraid. Look, your God is coming, vengeance is coming, the retribution of God; He is coming to save you. Then the eyes of the blind shall be opened, the ears of the deaf unsealed, then the lame shall leap like a deer and the tongues of the dumb sing for joy.* Is 35:4-6

4. Jesus Christ Is True Man

Jesus is a man like we are, having real flesh, a human body and soul. *The Word was made Flesh, He lived among us.* Jn 1:14. He experienced the joys and sorrows, pleasures and pains that you experience as a human being. Jesus is approachable because He is like you, a man. He understands your temptations, and your sins. Although He never sinned, He was tempted to sin: *Then Jesus was led by the Spirit out into the wilderness to be tempted by the devil.* Mt 4:1. He is like you in everything, except sin: *For it is not as if we had a high priest who was incapable of feeling our weaknesses with us; but we have One who has been tempted in every way that we are, though He is without sin.* Heb 4:15

5. Jesus Christ Is True God

St. John tells us that Jesus is God: *In the beginning was the Word, the Word was with God and the Word was God.* Jn 1:1. Jesus Christ said He was God; by His miracles He proved He was God.

Jesus said He was God before the chief priest when on trial for His life: *And the high priest said to Him, "I put You on oath by the living God to tell us if You are the Christ, the Son of God." "The words are your own" answered Jesus.* Mt 26:63-64

Christ showed He was Lord and Master of nature by several miracles like changing water into wine, multiplying loaves and fishes, calming a storm at sea, and by a miraculous catch of fish at sea. He was able to say: *But My testimony is greater than John's: the works My Father has given Me to carry out, these same works of Mine testify that the Father has sent Me.* Jn 5:36. At one time the Jews tried to stone Jesus to death because He said He was God: *The Jews fetched stones to stone Him, so Jesus said to them, "I have done many good works for you to see, works from My Father; for which of these are you stoning Me?" The Jews answered Him, "We are not stoning*

You for doing good work but for blasphemy: You are only a man and You claim to be God." Jn 10:31-34

Catholics with most other Christians accept Jesus Christ as True God, the Second Person of the Blessed Trinity. *Then Simon Peter spoke up, "You are the Christ," he said "the Son of the Living God."* Mt 16:17. It is Christ the man-God we receive in the Eucharist, Holy Communion; it is Christ God and man to Whom we go in the Scriptures; it is to Him with the Father and the Holy Spirit we pray. With St. John we call Christ *the Lamb of God that takes away the sin of the world.* Jn 1:29

6. Jesus Is The Most Perfect Man Who Ever Lived

Not only Christ's teaching but His life before the world was perfect. Jesus is a model of all virtues. He could say to the apostles and to us: *"Do you understand" He said "what I have done to you? You call me Master and Lord, and rightly; so I am. If I, then, the Lord and Master, have washed your feet, you should wash each other's feet. I have given you an example so that you may copy what I have done to you."* Jn 13:13-15. His life was without spot or stain: *Can one of you convict Me of sin?* Jn 8:45, He said. Christ's perfection will attract you to Him.

The depth of His perfection is manifested to us in His love for all mankind. He had a special tender love for the poor, the sick, and the sinners. *Come to Me, all you who labor and are overburdened, and I will give you rest. Shoulder My yoke and learn from Me, for I am gentle and humble in heart, and you will find rest for your souls. Yes, My yoke is easy and My burden light.* Mt 11:28-30

His love is recorded in the gospels in tender acts of compassion for people. Jesus had compassion on the widow of Naim:

> Now soon afterwards He went to a town called Naim, accompanied by His disciples and a great number of people. When He was near the gate of the town it happened that a dead man was being carried out for burial, the only son of his mother, and she was a widow. And a considerable number of the townspeople were with her. When the Lord saw her He felt sorry for her. "Do not cry" He said. Then He went up and

> put His hand on the bier and the bearers stood still, and He said, "Young man, I tell you to get up." And the dead man sat up and began to talk, and Jesus gave him to his mother. Everyone was filled with awe and praised God saying, "A great prophet has appeared among us; God has visited His people." Lk 7:11-16

Jesus loved sinners and forgave their sins. What greater act of forgiving love is there than Jesus forgiving even those who put Him to death when He said, *Father, forgive them; they do not know what they are doing.* Lk 23:34

Christ's perfection is clearly shown to us in His detachment from the goods of the world. So that He could give Himself to the Father and also attract us, He owned none of the things of the world: *Foxes have holes and the birds of the air have nests, but the Son of Man has nowhere to lay His head.* Mt 8:20. He was born in a stable. *And she gave birth to a Son, her first-born. She wrapped Him in swaddling clothes, and laid Him in a manger because there was no room for them at the inn.* Lk 2:7. In a beautiful manner He practiced what He teaches us about being overly concerned about the things of this world:

> That is why I am telling you not to worry about your life and what you are to eat, nor about your body and how you are to clothe it. Surely life means more than food, and the body more than clothing! Look at the birds in the sky. They do not sow or reap or gather into barns; yet your heavenly Father feeds them. Are you not worth much more than they are? Can any of you, for all his worrying, add one single cubit to his span of life? And why worry about clothing? Think of the flowers growing in the fields; they never have to work or spin; yet I assure you that not even Solomon in all his regalia was robed like one of these. Now if that is how God clothes the grass in the field which is there today and thrown into the furnace tomorrow, will He not much more look after you, you men of little faith? So do not worry; do not say, "What are we to eat? What are we to drink? How are we to be clothed?" It is the pagans who set their hearts on all these things. Your heavenly Father knows you need them all. Set your hearts on His kingdom first, and on His righteousness, and all these other things will be given you as well. So do not worry about tomorrow: tomorrow will take care of itself. Each day has enough trouble of its own. Mt 6:25-34

Christ invites each of us to the perfection of the Christian poverty He practiced: *Jesus said, "If you wish to be perfect, go and sell what you own and give the money to the poor, and you will have treasure in heaven; then come, follow Me."* Mt 19:21

Christ's perfection is shown to us in the way He gave Himself in prayer to the Father. Jesus prayed often and everywhere, in secret and in public. He often spent the whole night in prayer. *Now it was about this time that He went out into the hills to pray; and He spent the whole night in prayer to God.* Lk 6:12. Jesus spent forty days in the desert in praying and fasting: *Filled with the Holy Spirit, Jesus left the Jordan and was led by the Spirit through the wilderness, being tempted there by the devil for forty days.* Lk 4:1-2. Before performing miracles, Jesus prayed:

> Then Jesus lifted up His eyes and said: "Father, I thank You for hearing My prayer. I knew indeed that You always hear Me, but I speak for the sake of all these who stand round Me; so that they may believe it was You Who sent Me." When He had said this, He cried in a loud voice, "Lazarus, here! Come out!" The dead man came out, his feet and hands bound with bands of stuff and a cloth round his face. Jesus said to them, "Unbind him, let him go free." Jn 11:41-44

At the Last Supper, Jesus prayed for the apostles and for us: *I pray not only for these, but for those also who through their words will believe in Me. May they all be one. Father, may they be one in Us, as You are in Me and I am in You, so that the world may believe it was You who sent Me.* Jn 17:20-21

Christ's prayer for all of us teaches us not only His love for His Father and for us but also teaches us the necessity of prayer to God in our own lives.

7. Mary Is The Mother Of Jesus

Mary is truly the Mother of Jesus: *Listen! You are to conceive and bear a Son, and you must name Him Jesus. He will be great and will be called Son of the Most High.* Lk 1:31-32. Mary is the Mother of God because Jesus is God, the Second Person of the Blessed Trinity. Jesus Christ had no human father. As the Scriptures testify, Jesus was born of a virgin. St. Joseph and Mary lived the life of virginity. St. Joseph was the guardian of the Holy Family. Catholic teaching on Mary is clearly presented by the Second Vatican Council:

At the same time, however, she (Mary) belongs to the offspring of Adam; she is one with all human beings in their need for Salvation. Indeed she is "clearly the Mother of the members of Christ . . . since she cooperated out of love so that there might be born in the Church the faithful, who are members of Christ their Head." Therefore she is also hailed as a preeminent and altogether singular member of the Church, and as the Church's model and excellent exemplar in faith and charity. Taught by the Holy Spirit, the Catholic Church honors her with filial affection and piety as a most beloved mother.

Mary was involved in the mysteries of Christ. As the most holy Mother of God she was, after her Son, exalted by Divine grace above all angels and men. Hence the Church appropriately honors her with special reverence. Indeed, from most ancient times the Blessed Virgin has been venerated under the title of "God-bearer." In all perils and needs, the faithful have fled prayerfully to her protection. Especially after the Council of Ephesus the cult of the People of God toward Mary wonderfully increased in veneration and love, in invocation and imitation, according to her own prophetic words: "All generations shall call me blessed; because He Who is mighty has done great things for me." Lk 1:48

This most holy Synod deliberately teaches this Catholic doctrine. At the same time, it admonishes all the sons of the Church that the cult, especially the liturgical cult, of the Blessed Virgin, be generously fostered. It charges that practices and exercises of devotion toward her be treasured as recommended by the teaching authority of the Church in the course of centuries, and that those decrees issued in earlier times regarding the veneration of images of Christ, the Blessed Virgin, and the saints, be religiously observed.

Let them painstakingly guard against any word or deed which could lead separated brethren or anyone else into error regarding the true doctrine of the Church. Let the faithful remember moreover that true devotion consists neither in fruitless and passing emotion, nor in a certain vain credulity. Rather, it proceeds from true faith, by which we are led to know the excellence of the Mother of God, and are moved to a filial love toward our mother and to the imitation of her virtues. *Second Vatican Council*

CHRISTIAN PRACTICE

Read the Life of Jesus in the gospels.

Begin to practice Jesus' life of prayer by saying your morning and evening prayers.

Attend Mass every Sunday and pray and sing with the congregation.

CHRISTIAN PRAYER

O God, You have made this holy night radiant with Your own true brightness. Grant that we who have known the mystery of Christ's light on earth may also enjoy His happiness in heaven. *Mass at Christmas*

Almighty God, now that we have been enlightened by the Word made Flesh, grant that our deeds may reveal the light of faith that shines in our hearts. *Mass at Christmas*

Father, All-powerful and Ever-living God, we do well always and everywhere to give You thanks through Jesus Christ our Lord. In the wonder of the incarnation Your Eternal Word has brought to the eyes of faith a new and radiant vision of Your glory. In Him we see our God made visible and so are caught up in love of the God we cannot see. And so, with all the choirs of angels in heaven we proclaim Your glory and join in their unending hymn of praise. *Mass at Christmas*

Rejoice heartily, O daughter of Sion, shout for joy, O daughter of Jerusalem! See, your King shall come, a just Savior of the world is He. *Mass at Christmas*

SUGGESTED READING FROM SCRIPTURE

For when the fullness of time arrived, the Word was made flesh and dwelt among us in the fullness of grace and truth. *Second Vatican Council*

Gn 3:14-15 – In the Garden God promised mankind victory over Satan.
Is 64:1-12 – The prophet Isaiah prayed for the Redemption of his people and the remission of their sins.
Tt 3:1-8 – God shows His goodness toward us by sending the Savior.
Lk 2:41-52 – Christ's dedication to the Father.
Mk 1:35-39 – Jesus at prayer.
Jn 8:48-59 – Jesus obedient to the Father.
Mt 19:16-21 – Jesus invites all to the life of perfection.
Lk 15:4-7 – Jesus' story about the Lost Sheep.
Jn 13:33-38; 14:1-31; 15:1-27; 16:1-33; 17:1-26 – Jesus' talk at the Last Supper in which the Savior's soul is opened to us.

Lesson 7: JESUS CHRIST OUR TEACHER

1. Jesus Christ Was Sent By God The Father To Teach Us

Jesus Christ was sent by God the Father to teach us. Jesus taught with the authority of God: *Jesus had now finished what He wanted to say, and His teaching made a deep impression on the people because He taught them with authority, and not like their own scribes.* Mt 7:28-29. He taught more with the authority of God's truth than with discussion or reasoning. *There has never been anybody who has spoken like Him.* Jn 7:46. About His teaching Jesus said: *Heaven and earth will pass away, but My words will never pass away.* Mt 24:35. Jesus said:

> Therefore, everyone who listens to these words of Mine and acts on them will be like a sensible man who built his house on rock. Rain came down, floods rose, gales blew and hurled themselves against that house, and it did not fall: it was founded on rock. But everyone who listens to these words of Mine and does not act on them will be like a stupid man who built his house on sand. Rain came down, floods rose, gales blew and struck that house, and it fell; and what a fall it had! Mt 7:24-27

2. Christ Teaches Us In Clear Sermons And Stories

Christ's words are easy to understand. His stories, parables, are full of heavenly doctrine breathing a tender love of God and man.

3. The Principal Teaching Of Jesus Is Love Of God And Love Of Neighbor

Jesus teaches us: *You must love the Lord your God with all your heart, with all your soul, and with all your mind. This is the greatest and the first commandment. The second resembles it: You must love your neighbor as yourself. On these two commandments hang the whole Law, and the prophets also.* Mt 22:37-40

4. Jesus Teaches Us To Love The Father By Giving Us An Example Of His Perfect Love Of The Father

Christ showed loving obedience to God the Father:

> In your minds you must be the same as Christ Jesus. His state was Divine, yet He did not cling to His equality with God but emptied Himself to assume the condition of a slave, and be-

came as men are; and being as all men are, He was humbler yet, even to accepting death, death on a cross. But God raised Him high and gave Him the name which is above all other names so that all beings in the heavens, on earth and in the underworld, should bend the knee at the name of Jesus and that every tongue should acclaim Jesus Christ as Lord, to the glory of God the Father. Ph 2:5-11

To teach us love of the Father, Jesus did what was pleasing to God the Father: *When you have lifted up the Son of Man, then you will know that I am He and that I do nothing of Myself: what the Father has taught Me is what I preach; He Who sent Me is with Me, and has not left Me to Myself, for I always do what pleases Him.* Jn 8:28-29

By His own example Jesus teaches us to do the will of the Father: *My food is to do the will of the One Who sent Me, and to complete His work.* Jn 4:34

You should try to love the Father as Jesus does by living the life that He teaches: *You must therefore be perfect just as your heavenly Father is perfect.* Mt 5:48

5. In Many Ways Jesus Teaches Us To Love All People

In the story of the Good Samaritan Jesus teaches us to love all, even strangers:

> A man was once on his way down from Jerusalem to Jericho and fell into the hands of brigands; they took all he had, beat him and then made off, leaving him half dead. Now a priest happened to be traveling down the same road, but when he saw the man, he passed by on the other side. In the same way a Levite who came to the place saw him, and passed by on the other side. But a Samaritan traveler who came upon him was moved with compassion when he saw him. He went up and bandaged his wounds, pouring oil and wine on them. He then lifted him on to his own mount, carried him to the inn and looked after him. Lk 10:30-34

Jesus teaches us to love even our enemies: *But I say this to you: love your enemies and pray for those who persecute you; in this way you will be sons of your Father in heaven, for He causes His sun to rise on bad men as well as good, and His rain to fall on honest and dishonest men alike. For if you love those who love you, what right have you to claim any credit? Even the tax collectors do as much, do they not?* Mt 5:44-46

In the story of the unmerciful servant, Jesus teaches us to forgive our enemies even as God forgives us:

> And so the kingdom of heaven may be compared to a king who decided to settle his accounts with his servants. When the reckoning began, they brought him a man who owed ten thousand talents; but he had no means of paying, so his master gave orders that he should be sold, together with his wife and children and all his possessions, to meet the debt. At this, the servant threw himself down at his master's feet. "Give me time" he said "and I will pay the whole sum." And the servant's master felt so sorry for him that he let him go and canceled the debt. Now as this servant went out, he happened to meet a fellow servant who owed him one hundred denarii; and he seized him by the throat and began to throttle him. "Pay what you owe me" he said. His fellow servant fell at his feet and implored him, saying, "Give me time and I will pay you." But the other would not agree; on the contrary, he had him thrown into prison till he should pay the debt. His fellow servants were deeply distressed when they saw what had happened, and they went to their master and reported the whole affair to him. Then the master sent for him. "You wicked servant," he said "I canceled all that debt of yours when you appealed to me. Were you not bound, then, to have pity on your fellow servant just as I had pity on you?" And in his anger the master handed him over to the torturers till he should pay all his debt. And that is how my heavenly Father will deal with you unless you each forgive your brother from your heart. Mt 18:23-35

6. Jesus Teaches Us To Love All With Sincere Heart When He Teaches Us How God Loves All People Who Are In Trouble Especially Sinners

Christ teaches us to love sinners. He said:

> A man had two sons. The younger said to his father, "Father, let me have the share of the estate that would come to me". So the father divided the property between them. A few days later, the younger son got together everything he had and left for a distant country where he squandered his money on a life of debauchery. When he had spent it all, that country experienced a severe famine, and now he began to feel the pinch, so he hired himself out to one of the local inhabitants who put him on his farm to feed the pigs. And he would willingly have filled his belly with the husks the pigs were eating but no one offered him anything. Then he came to his senses and said, "How many of my father's paid servants have more food than they want, and here am I dying of hunger! I will leave this place and go to my father and say: 'Father, I have sinned

against heaven and against you; I no longer deserve to be called your son; treat me as one of your paid servants.'" So he left the place and went back to his father. While he was still a long way off, his father saw him and was moved with pity. He ran to the boy, clasped him in his arms and kissed him tenderly. Then his son said, "Father, I have sinned against heaven and against you. I no longer deserve to be called your son." But the father said to his servants, "Quick! Bring out the best robe and put it on him; put a ring on his finger and sandals on his feet. Bring the calf we have been fattening, and kill it; we are going to have a feast, a celebration, because this son of mine was dead and has come back to life; he was lost and is found." And they began to celebrate. Lk 15:11-24

By telling us that He died for sinners Jesus is also teaching us to love all, even sinners: *A man can have no greater love than to lay down his life for his friends.* Jn 15:13

By referring to Himself as the Good Shepherd, Jesus is teaching us to love all people:

I am the Good Shepherd: The Good Shepherd is one who lays down his life for his sheep. The hired man, since he is not the shepherd and the sheep do not belong to him, abandons the sheep and runs away as soon as he sees a wolf coming, and then the wolf attacks and scatters the sheep; this is because he is only a hired man and has no concern for the sheep. I am the Good Shepherd; I know My own and My own know Me, just as the Father knows Me and I know the Father; and I lay down My life for My sheep. Jn 10:11-15

By teaching us His tender love for the sick, Jesus teaches us to have tender compassion for all who are in trouble: *The blind see again, the lame walk, lepers are cleansed, and the deaf hear.* Lk 7:22. When He invites all who are in difficulty to come to Him, Jesus is also teaching us to love all: *Come to Me, all you who labor and are overburdened, and I will give you rest. Shoulder My yoke and learn from Me, for I am gentle and humble in heart, and you will find rest for your souls. Yes, My yoke is easy and My burden light.* Mt 11:28-30

7. Jesus Teaches Us Today

Jesus Christ today teaches us through the Scriptures and through the Catholic Church. In a future lesson we shall see that Jesus established His Church upon earth to carry on all His works including the work of teaching the world His doctrine.

CHRISTIAN PRACTICE

Read the parables of Jesus and try to understand the lesson He is trying to bring to you in each parable.

Love all even as Jesus did; associate with people of other races and religions.

Begin to practice acts of love toward the sick and the old people in your neighborhood.

Visit those in prison.

Attend wakes and funerals and pray for the dead.

Try not to talk badly about people you do not like.

CHRISTIAN PRAYER

I believe in God, the Father Almighty, Creator of heaven and earth; and in Jesus Christ, His only Son, our Lord; Who was conceived by the Holy Spirit, born of the Virgin Mary, suffered under Pontius Pilate, was crucified, died, and was buried. He descended into hell; the third day He arose again from the dead; He ascended into heaven, sits at the right hand of God, the Father Almighty; from thence He shall come to judge the living and the dead. I believe in the Holy Spirit, the holy Catholic Church, the communion of saints, the forgiveness of sins, the resurrection of the body, and life everlasting. Amen. *The Apostles' Creed*

SUGGESTED READING FROM SCRIPTURE

Jesus Christ, therefore, the Word made Flesh, sent as a man to men, speaks the words of God. *Second Vatican Council*

Lk 10:30-37 – The Good Samaritan.
Mt 18:21-35 – The Merciless Servant.
Lk 16:19-31 – The Greedy Rich Man.
Mt 5:1-12 – The sermon on the mountain, the whole Christian teaching.
Mt 13:24-43 – Good people and evil people in the Church.
Lk 7:36-50 – The Forgiven Debtors.
Lk 13:1-9 – Examples inviting us to repentance.
Mk 12:1-12 – The Wicked Husbandmen.
Lk 18:1-8 – The Persistent Widow.
Mt 20:1-16 – Laborers in the Vineyard.
Mt 13:1-52 – Jesus speaks in Parables.
Lk 18:9-14 – The Pharisee and the Publican.
Lk 19:11-27 – The Pounds.
Lk 15:11-32 – The Prodigal Son.
Lk 12:16-21 – The Foolish Rich Man.
Mt 24:44-51 – The Good and Bad Servants.
Lk 15:1-7 – The Lost Sheep.
Jn 10:1-21 – The Good Shepherd.
Mt 21:28-32 – The Two Sons.
Mt 13:3-23 – The Sower and the Seed.
Lk 16:1-8 – The Unjust Steward.
Lk 14:16-24 – The Great Supper.
Mt 25:14-30 – The Talents.
Mt 13:44 – The Treasure Hidden in a Field.
Mt 25:1-13 – The Wise and Foolish Virgins.

Lesson 8: JESUS CHRIST DIED ON THE CROSS FOR YOU AND FOR ALL MANKIND

1. Jesus Died For Your Sins

Jesus Christ in His perfect love for you died on the cross to make up for your personal sins and to regain for you the life of grace and to make up for the sin of Adam. *Yet He was pierced through for our faults, crushed for our sins. On Him lies a punishment that brings us peace, and through His wounds we are healed.* Is 53:5. Christ is our mediator with God: *For there is only one God, and there is only one mediator between God and mankind, Himself a man, Jesus Christ, Who sacrificed Himself as a ransom for them all.* 1 Tm 2:5-6. Paul reminds us of what Christ by His death has done for us: *Because that is what He has done: He has taken us out of the power of darkness and created a place for us in the kingdom of the Son that He loves, and in Him, we gain our freedom, the forgiveness of our sins.* Col 1:13-14

Sin is an offense against God. Only God can forgive our sins. God chose His Son to be the one to suffer and to die for our sins. *Bulls' blood and goats' blood are useless for taking away sins.* Heb 10:4. Jesus is called Our Savior because He saved us from sin. He is called Redeemer because He paid the price for us; He bought us back. *As by one man's disobedience many were made sinners, so by one man's obedience many will be made righteous.* Rm 5:19

2. The Suffering Of Our Lord, Jesus Christ, According To St. Matthew

As we do on Palm Sunday we now take the suffering of Our Lord Jesus Christ from St. Matthew in the Scriptures.

Jesus' Suffering And Prayer In The Garden Of Gethsemane

Then Jesus came with them to a small estate called Gethsemane; and He said to His disciples, "Stay here while I go over there to pray." He took Peter and the two sons of Zebedee with Him. And sadness came over Him, and great distress. Then He said to them, "My soul is sorrowful to the point of death. Wait here and keep awake with Me." And going on a little further He fell on His face and prayed. "My Father," He said "if it is possible, let this cup pass Me by. Nevertheless, let it be as You, not I, would have it." He came back to the disciples and found them sleeping, and He said to Peter, "So you had not the strength to keep awake with Me one hour? You should be awake, and praying not to be put to the test. The spirit is willing, but the flesh is weak." Again, a second time, He went away and prayed: "My Father," He said "if this cup cannot pass by without My drinking it, Your will be done!" And He came back again and found them sleeping, their eyes were so heavy. Leaving them there, He went away again and prayed for the third time, repeating the same words. Then He came back to the disciples and said to them, "You can sleep on now and take your rest. Now the hour has come when the Son of Man is to be betrayed into the hands of sinners. Get up! Let us go! My betrayer is already close at hand."

Judas And The Crowd Come To Arrest Jesus

He was still speaking when Judas, one of the Twelve, appeared, and with him a large number of men armed with swords and clubs, sent by the chief priests and elders of the people. Now the traitor had arranged a sign with them. "The one I kiss," he had said "He is the man. Take Him in charge." So he went straight up to Jesus and said, "Greetings, Rabbi," and kissed Him. Jesus said to him, "My friend, do what you are here for." Then they came forward, seized Jesus and took Him in charge.

The Disciples Run Away

At that, one of the followers of Jesus grasped his sword and drew it; he struck out at the high priest's servant, and cut off his ear. Jesus then said, "Put your sword back, for all who draw the sword will die by the sword. Or do you think that I cannot appeal to My Father Who would promptly send more than twelve legions of angels to my defense? But then, how would the Scriptures be fulfilled that say this is the way it must be?" It was at this time that Jesus said to the crowds, "Am I a brigand, that you had to set out to capture Me with swords and clubs? I sat teaching in the Temple day after day and you never laid hands on Me." Now all this happened to fulfill the prophecies in Scripture. Then all the disciples deserted Him and ran away.

Jesus Is Taken Before The Sanhedrin

The men who had arrested Jesus led Him off to Caiaphas the high priest where the scribes and the elders were assembled. Peter followed Him at a distance, and when He reached the high priest's palace, he went in and sat down with the attendants to see what the end would be. The chief priests and the whole Sanhedrin were looking for evidence against Jesus, however false, on which they might pass the death-sentence. But they could not find any, though several lying witnesses came forward. Eventually two stepped forward and made a statement, "This Man said, 'I have power to destroy the Temple of God and in three days build it up.'"

Jesus Proclaims His Divinity

The high priest then stood up and said to Him, "Have You no answer to that? What is this evidence these men are bringing against You?" But Jesus was silent. And the high priest said to Him, "I put You on oath by the living God to tell us if You are the Christ the Son of God." "The words are your own" answered Jesus. "Moreover, I tell you that from this time onward you will see the Son of Man seated at the right hand of the Power and coming on the clouds of heaven." At this, the high priest tore His clothes and said, "He has blasphemed. What need of witnesses have we now? There! You have just heard the blasphemy. What is your opinion?" They answered, "He deserves to die." Then they spat in His face and hit Him with their fists; others said as they struck Him, "Play the prophet, Christ! Who hit You then?"

Peter Denies Christ

Meanwhile Peter was sitting outside in the courtyard, and a servant-girl came up to him and said, "You too were with Jesus the Galilean." But he denied it in front of them all. "I do not know what you are talking about" he said. When he went out to the gateway another servant-girl saw him and said to the people there, "This man was with Jesus the Nazarene." And again, with an oath, he denied it, "I do not know the Man." A little later the bystanders came up and said to Peter, "You are one of them for sure! Why, your accent gives you away." Then he started calling down curses on himself and swearing, "I do not know the Man." At that moment the cock crew, and Peter remembered what Jesus had said, "Before the cock crows you will have disowned Me three times." And he went outside and wept bitterly.

Jesus Is Led Before Pilate

When morning came, all the chief priests and the elders of the people met in council to bring about the death of Jesus. They had Him bound, and led Him away to hand Him over to Pilate, the governor.

Suicide—Judas Kills Himself

When he found that Jesus had been condemned, Judas His betrayer was filled with remorse and took the thirty silver pieces back to the chief priests and elders. "I have sinned;" he said "I have betrayed innocent blood." "What is that to us?" they replied "That is your concern." And flinging down the silver pieces in the sanctuary he made off, and went and hanged himself.

Jesus Before Pilate

Jesus, then, was brought before the governor, and the governor put to him this question. "Are you the king of the Jews?" Jesus replied, "It is you who say it." But when He was accused by the chief priests and the elders He refused to answer at all. Pilate then said to Him, "Do you not hear how many charges they have brought against You?" But to the governor's complete amazement, He offered no reply to any of the charges. At festival time it was the governor's practice to release a prisoner for the people, anyone they chose. Now there was at that time a notorious prisoner whose name was Barabbas. So when the crowd gathered, Pilate said to them, "Which do you want me to release for you: Barabbas, or Jesus Who is called Christ?" For Pilate knew it was out of jealousy that they had handed Him over. Now as he was seated in the chair of judgment, his wife sent him a message, "Have nothing to do with that Man; I have been upset all day by a dream I had about Him." The chief priests and the elders, however, had persuaded the crowd to demand the release of Barabbas and the execution of Jesus. So when the governor spoke and asked them, "Which of the two do you want me to release for you?" they said, "Barabbas." "But in that case," Pilate said to them "what am I to do with Jesus Who is called Christ?" They all said, "Let Him be crucified!" "Why?" he asked "What harm has He done?" But they shouted all the louder, "Let Him be crucified!" Then Pilate saw that he was making no impression, that in fact a riot was imminent. So he took some water, washed his hands in front of the crowd and said, "I am innocent of this Man's blood. It is your concern." And the people, to a man, shouted back, "His blood be on us and on our children!" Then he released Barabbas for them. He ordered Jesus to be first scourged and then handed over to be crucified.

Jesus Is Crowned With Thorns

The governor's soldiers took Jesus with them into the Praetorium and collected the whole cohort round Him. Then they stripped Him and made Him wear a scarlet cloak, and having twisted some thorns into a crown they put this on His head and placed a reed in His right hand. To make fun of Him they knelt to Him saying, "Hail, King of the Jews." And they spat on Him and took the reed and struck Him on the head with it. And when they had finished making fun of Him, they took off the cloak and dressed Him in His own clothes and led Him away to crucify Him.

Jesus Is Crucified

On their way out, they came across a man from Cyrene, Simon by name, and enlisted him to carry His cross. When they had reached a place called Golgotha, that is, the place of the skull, they gave Him wine to drink mixed with gall, which He tasted but refused to drink. When they had finished crucifying Him they shared out His clothing by casting lots, and then sat down and stayed there keeping guard over Him. Above His head was placed the charge against Him; it read: "This is Jesus, the King of the Jews." At the same time two robbers were crucified with Him, one on the right and one on the left.

Jesus Dies On The Cross For Our Sins

From the sixth hour there was darkness over all the land until the ninth hour. And about the ninth hour, Jesus cried out in a loud voice, "Eli, Eli, lama sabachthani?" that is, "My God, My God, why have You deserted Me?" When some of those who stood there heard this, they said, "The Man is calling on Elijah," and one of them quickly ran to get a sponge which he dipped in vinegar and, putting it on a reed, gave Him to drink. "Wait!" said the rest of them "and see if Elijah will come to save Him." But Jesus, again crying out in a loud voice, yielded up His spirit.

The Burial Of Jesus

When it was evening, there came a rich man of Arimathaea, called Joseph, who had himself become a disciple of Jesus. This man went to Pilate and asked for the Body of Jesus. Pilate thereupon ordered it to be handed over. So Joseph took the body, wrapped it in a clean shroud and put it in his own new tomb which he had hewn out of rock. He then rolled a large stone across the entrance of the tomb and went away. Now Mary of Magdala and the other Mary were there, sitting opposite the sepulchre. Mt 26:36-75 to Mt 27:1-61

3. Lessons To Be Learned From The Suffering And Death of Jesus

From a prayerful reading of the suffering and death of Jesus you should realize how much God loves you, how terrible sin is in the eyes of God Who demanded such suffering from His Son to atone for sin.

> Yes, God loved the world so much that He gave His only Son, so that everyone who believes in Him may not be lost but may have eternal life. For God sent His Son into the world not to condemn the world, but so that through Him the world might be saved. Jn 3:16-17

You should realize the debt of gratitude you owe Christ. *Since God did not spare His Own Son, but gave Him up to benefit us all.* Rm 8:32. You should make a sincere resolution as you gaze on the cross of Christ to avoid all sin and whatever leads to sin. More positively you should give yourself and your service to Christ and His Church thus participating daily in the Sacrifice of Calvary.

Father, All-powerful and Ever-living God, we do well always and everywhere to give You thanks. You decreed that man should be saved through the wood of the cross. The tree of man's defeat became his tree of victory; where life was lost, there life has been restored through Christ our Lord. *Preface of the Holy Cross from the Mass*

4. The Sacrifice Of Jesus On The Cross Is Re-Presented Or Repeated At Every Mass

Jesus is offered in sacrifice every time a priest offers the Sacrifice of the Mass. *But from farthest east to farthest west My name is honored among the nations and everywhere a sacrifice of incense is offered to My Name, and a pure offering too, since My Name is honored among the nations, says Yahweh Sabaoth.* Ml 1:11

The same priest, Jesus Christ, the same offering, Christ's Body and Blood, is offered to God for all of us at each Mass celebrated in the Catholic Church. For it is through the liturgy, especially the Divine Eucharistic Sacrifice, that the work of our Redemption is exercised. Second Vatican Council

A sacrifice is the offering of a gift to God, by a priest, in order to honor God as the Lord of Creation. In Mass, the re-presentation of the cross, we honor God, we thank God, we beg God for His help, we get pardon for our sins and we offer ourselves to God with the Christian community.

CHRISTIAN PRACTICE

Have a Crucifix in your home in a place of honor: *Behold the wood of the cross upon which hung the Savior of the world.*

Pray the Stations of the Cross in your parish Church: *We adore You, O Christ, and we bless You, because by Your holy cross You have redeemed the world.*

Do not take your sins lightly. Remember, you added to the burden of Christ.

Resolve to avoid sin in the future: *They cannot be repentant if they have wilfully crucified the Son of God and openly mocked Him.* Heb 6:6

Take to heart the Church speaking for Christ: *O My people, what have I done to you? In what have I offended you? Answer Me.*

Remember our Lord with love and sympathy for the wounds suffered for you.

Everytime you offer Mass remember that you are offering Christ Who died for you.

CHRISTIAN PRAYER

My people, what have I done to you? or how have I offended you? Answer Me. Because I led you out of the land of Egypt, you have prepared a cross for your Savior. Holy God. Holy God. Holy, Mighty One. Holy, Mighty One. Holy, Immortal One, have mercy on us. Holy, Immortal One, have mercy on us. Because I led you out through the desert forty years, and fed you with manna, and brought you into a very good land, you have prepared a cross for your Savior. Holy God. Holy God. Holy, Mighty One. Holy, Mighty One. Holy, Immortal One, have mercy on us. Holy, Immortal One, have mercy on us. What more should I have done, and did not? Behold I have planted you as My fairest vine, and you have become very bitter to Me, for you have quenched My thirst with vinegar, and with a lance you have pierced your Savior's side. Holy God. Holy God, Holy, Mighty One. Holy, Mighty One. Holy, Immortal One, have mercy on us. Holy, Immortal One, have mercy on us. *Reproaches of Good Friday*

O Lord, let your rich blessing descend upon Your people who again commemorate the passion and death of Your Son. Grant us pardon and peace; increase our faith and make certain our eternal Redemption. Through Christ our Lord. Amen.

Almighty and merciful God, You have healed us by the holy passion and death of Christ. Be ever merciful to us and grant that we may always live a holy life by sharing in this mystery. Through Christ our Lord. Amen.

Lamb of God, You take away the sins of the world, have mercy on us. *The Mass*

SUGGESTED READING FROM SCRIPTURE

For this reason Jesus perfected Revelation by fulfilling it through His whole work of making Himself present and manifesting Himself: through

His words and deeds, His signs and wonders, but especially through His death and glorious Resurrection from the dead and final sending of the Spirit of truth. *Second Vatican Council*

Is 53:2-12 – Isaiah the prophet tells how Christ's love for us led Him to be victim for our sins.

Zc 11:10-14 – The prophecy concerning the treachery of Judas.

Ps 54:1-7; 55:1-23; 56:1-11; 57:1-11 – David foretells fear and horror in the soul of Jesus.

Ps 27:11-14 – David foretells the false witnesses against the Messias.

Ps 22:6-7 – David foretells the suffering of Jesus, a worm rather than a man.

Ps 69:21 – David foretells of the gall and vinegar given to the insulted dying Savior.

Ep 1:3-10 – We have Redemption in the Blood of Christ, remission of sins, according to the riches of His grace.

Lesson 9: JESUS AROSE FROM THE DEAD AND ASCENDED INTO HEAVEN

1. Jesus Arose From The Dead

The Resurrection of Jesus Christ is recorded in the Scriptures:

> After the sabbath, and towards dawn on the first day of the week, Mary of Magdala and the other Mary went to visit the sepulchre. And all at once there was a violent earthquake, for the angel of the Lord, descending from heaven, came and rolled away the stone and sat on it. His face was like lightning, his robe white as snow. The guards were so shaken, so frightened of him, that they were like dead men. But the angel spoke; and he said to the women, "There is no need for you to be afraid. I know you are looking for Jesus, Who was crucified. He is not here, for He has risen, as He said He would. Come and see the place where He lay, then go quickly and tell His disciples . . . 'He has risen from the dead and now He is going before you to Galilee; it is there you will see Him.' Now I have told you." . . . And there, coming to meet them, was Jesus. "Greetings" He said. And the women came up to Him and, falling down before Him, clasped His feet. Then Jesus said to them, "Do not be afraid; go and tell My brothers that they must leave for Galilee; they will see Me there." While they were on their way, some of the guard went off into the city to tell the chief priests all that had happened. These held a meeting with the elders and, after some discussion, handed a considerable sum of money to the soldiers with these instructions, "This is what you must say, 'His disciples came during the night and stole Him away while we were asleep.' And should the governor come to hear of this, we undertake to put things right with Him ourselves and to see that you do not get into trouble." The soldiers took the money and carried out their instructions, and to this day that is the story among the Jews. Meanwhile the eleven disciples set out for Galilee, to the mountain where Jesus had arranged to meet them. When they saw Him they fell down before Him, though some hesitated. Jesus came up and spoke to them. He said, "All authority, in heaven and on earth has been given to Me. Go, therefore, make disciples of all the nations; baptize them in the name of the Father and of the Son and of the Holy Spirit, and teach them to observe all the commands I gave you. And know that I am with you always; yes, to the end of time." Mt 28:1-20

St. Paul tells us of the glorious fact of the Resurrection of Jesus from the dead:

> Well then, in the first place, I taught you what I had been taught myself, namely that Christ died for our sins, in accordance with the Scriptures; that He was buried; and that He was raised to life on the third day, in accordance with the Scriptures; that He appeared first to Cephas and secondly to the Twelve. Next He appeared to more than five hundred of the brothers at the same time, most of whom are still alive, though some have died; then He appeared to James, and then to all the apostles; and last of all He appeared to me too; it was as though I was born when no one expected it. I am the least of the apostles; in fact, since I persecuted the Church of God, I hardly deserve the name apostle; but by God's grace that is what I am, and the grace that He gave me has not been fruitless. On the contrary, I, or rather the grace of God that is with me, have worked harder than any of the others; but what matters is that I preach what they preach, and this is what you all believed. 1 Co 15:3-11

2. By His Resurrection Jesus Proves He Is The Son Of God

The entrance hymn for the Mass on Easter Sunday brings the following joyful message to Christian hearts: *I arose, and am still with You, alleluia; You rest Your hand upon me, alleluia; Your knowledge is too wonderful, alleluia, alleluia. O Lord, You have probed me and You know me; You know when I sit and when I stand.* By conquering death through His own power, Christ has shown Himself Master of life and death; therefore, Jesus the Son of God, the Second Person of the Blessed Trinity is true God as well as true man. *And if Christ has not been raised then our preaching is useless and your believing it is useless*; 1 Co 15:14, says St. Paul. Christ has manifested Himself as the King of Kings and Lord of Lords, your personal Savior.

> His empire shall stretch from sea to sea, from the river to the ends of the earth. The Beast will cower before Him and His enemies grovel in the dust; the kings of Tarshish and of the islands will pay Him tribute. The kings of Sheba and Seba will offer gifts; all kings will do Him homage, all nations become His servants. Ps 72:8-11

3. Christ's Resurrection Brings Us From The Death Of Sin To The Life Of Grace

Through Baptism Jesus brings us from the death of sin to the life of grace. *He is the true Lamb Who took away the sins of the world. By dying He destroyed our death; by rising He restored our life. Easter Vigil. O God You make this whole night radiant with the glory of the Resurrection of our Lord. Preserve in the new members of your family the spirit of sonship that You have conferred on them, so that they may be made new in body and soul to render You singlehearted service.* Mass on Easter

Baptized Christians resolve with St. Paul to seek the things of God:

> Since you have been brought back to true life with Christ, you must look for the things that are in heaven, where Christ is, sitting at God's right hand. Let your thoughts be on heavenly things, not on the things that are on the earth, because you have died, and now the life you have is hidden with Christ in God. But when Christ is revealed—and He is your life—you too will be revealed in all your glory with Him. Col 3:1-4

United to Christ we should try to avoid sin because of Christ's Resurrection and our Baptism:

> Does it follow that we should remain in sin so as to let grace have greater scope? Of course not. We are dead in sin, so how can we continue to live in it? You have been taught that when we were baptized in Christ Jesus we were baptized in His death; in other words, when we were baptized we went into the tomb with Him and joined Him in death, so that as Christ was raised from the dead by the Father's glory, we too might live a new life. If in union with Christ we have imitated His death, we shall also imitate Him in His Resurrection. We must realize that our former selves have been crucified with Him to destroy this sinful body and to free us from the slavery of sins. When a man dies, of course, he has finished with sin. Rm 6:1-7
>
> Blessed be God the Father of our Lord Jesus Christ, Who in His great mercy has given us a new birth as His sons, by raising Jesus Christ from the dead, so that we have a sure hope and the promise of an inheritance that can never be spoilt or soiled and never fade away, because it is being kept for you in the heavens. Through your faith, God's power will guard you until the Salvation which has been prepared is revealed at the end of time. This is a cause of great joy for

you, even though you may for a short time have to bear being plagued by all sorts of trials; so that, when Jesus Christ is revealed, your faith will have been tested and proved like gold—only it is more precious than gold, which is corruptible even though it bears testing by fire—and then you will have praise and glory and honor. You did not see Him, yet you love Him; and still without seeing Him, you are already filled with a joy so glorious that it cannot be described, because you believe; and you are sure of the end to which your faith looks forward, that is, the Salvation of your souls. It was this Salvation that the prophets were looking and searching so hard for; their prophecies were about the grace which was to come to you. The spirit of Christ which was in them foretold the sufferings of Christ and the glories that would come after them, and they tried to find out at what time and in what circumstances all this was to be expected. It was revealed to them that the news they brought of all the things which have now been announced to you, by those who preached to you the Good News through the Holy Spirit sent from heaven, was for you and not for themselves. Even the angels long to catch a glimpse of these things. Free your minds, then, of encumbrances; control them, and put your trust in nothing but the grace that will be given you when Jesus Christ is revealed. I P 1:3-14

4. The Celebration Of Jesus' Resurrection In The Easter Vigil

The Resurrection of Jesus with its deep meaning for your life and the life of every Christian is brought clearly, dramatically and prayerfully to us in the Easter Vigil Service in the Catholic Church. In it Christ's passage from death to life and our passage from the death of sin to life in Christ is clearly taught to us. New water, new fire, new light teaches the newness of life that the Christian receives in Baptism. Those recently instructed in the Catholic Faith are given the new life of grace in Baptism on this night. The Mass of the Resurrection is celebrated with heartfelt Christian joy. Easter is truly the greatest of the Church's feast days.

5. Jesus Ascends Into Heaven

Jesus' Ascension into heaven is beautifully and clearly recorded in the Acts of the Apostles:

In my earlier work, Theophilus, I dealt with everything Jesus had done and taught from the beginning until the day He gave His instructions to the apostles He had chosen through the Holy Spirit, and was taken up to heaven. He had shown Himself alive to them after His passion by many demonstrations: for forty days He had continued to appear to them and tell them about the kingdom of God. When He had been at table with them, He had told them not to leave Jerusalem, but to wait there for what the Father had promised. "It is" He had said "what you have heard Me speak about: John baptized with water but you, not many days from now, will be baptized with the Holy Spirit." Now having met together, they asked Him, "Lord, has the time come? Are You going to restore the kingdom to Israel?" He replied, "It is not for you to know times or dates that the Father has decided by His own authority, but you will receive power when the Holy Spirit comes on you, and then you will be My witnesses not only in Jerusalem but throughout Judaea and Samaria, and indeed to the ends of the earth."

As He said this He was lifted up while they looked on, and a cloud took Him from their sight. They were still staring into the sky when suddenly two men in white were standing near them and they said, "Why are you men from Galilee standing here looking into the sky? Jesus Who has been taken up from You into heaven, this same Jesus will come back in the same way as you have seen Him go there." Ac 1:1-11

Jesus Christ, equal to the Father in power and majesty, awaits us in heaven. Christ in heaven is our King awaiting our glorious resurrection and ascension.

To prepare us for our resurrection and ascension, Jesus asks us to make Him King of our minds by accepting Him as the Truth, King of our wills by our obedience to His laws, and King of our hearts by accepting the love He offers us. *For us, our homeland is in heaven, and from heaven comes the Savior we are waiting for, the Lord Jesus Christ, and He will transfigure these wretched bodies of ours into copies of His glorious Body.* Ph 3:20

CHRISTIAN PRACTICE

But, as the Apostle teaches us, we have by Baptism been buried with Christ into death. As Christ, then, has risen from the dead, so we too must walk now in newness of life. For we know that our old self has been crucified with Christ, that we may no longer be slaves to sin. Let us remember always that we have died to sin, but are to live for God, in Christ Jesus our Lord. *Easter Vigil*

CHRISTIAN PRAYER

It is of this night that Scripture says: "And the night shall be as bright as day. And the night shall light up my joy." The holiness of this night removes all wickedness and washes away sin and restores innocence to those who have fallen. It puts hatred to flight, brings peace and humbles pride. *Easter Vigil*

O Almighty God, we firmly believe that Your Only-begotten Son, our Redeemer, ascended this day into heaven. May our minds dwell always on this heavenly home. *Mass of Ascension Thursday*

SUGGESTED READING FROM SCRIPTURE

In His goodness and wisdom, God chose to reveal Himself and to make known to us the hidden purpose of His will by which through Christ, the Word made Flesh, man has access to the Father in the Holy Spirit and comes to share in the Divine nature. *Second Vatican Council*

- Ep 2:1-10 – Through the Resurrection of Jesus we pass from the death of sin to the life of Christ.
- 1 Th 4:13-18 – After death, we share in Christ's Easter victory to the fullest.
- Jn 20:1-31; 21:1-14 – Mary Magdalen and the apostles see Jesus after His Resurrection.
- Lk 24:13-32 – The Risen Lord shows Himself to the disciples at Emmaus.
- Mt 28:16-20 – Jesus appears before His glorious Ascension into heaven and sends the apostles to make disciples of all nations.
- Lk 19:12-28 – Jesus hints at His own Ascension when He told the story of the nobleman who went on a long journey in order to receive the kingdom.
- Ac 1:1-11 – Christ ascends into heaven in the presence of His apostles.
- Heb 9:24-28 – Jesus Who is in heaven will return to judge us.

1. Grateful Love And Thanksgiving Urges You To Adore God

From a realization of God's love for you, your complete dependence upon God and your possession of God's life through Baptism, you ought to feel a deep and grateful love of God. You want to give Him the highest honor and praise: *Come, let us praise Yahweh joyfully, acclaiming the Rock of our safety; let us come into His presence with thanksgiving, acclaiming Him with music.* Ps 95:6-7. You want to give God thanks in the most perfect way you can give thanks: *Yahweh, I am Your servant, Your servant, son of a pious mother, You undo my fetters. I will offer you the thanksgiving sacrifice, invoking the name of Yahweh.* Ps 116:16-17. You want to tell God you are sorry for your sins and want to remain His child through the adoption of grace: *Have mercy on me, O God, in Your goodness, in Your great tenderness wipe away my faults; wash me clean of my guilt, purify me from my sin . . . do not banish me from Your presence, do not deprive me of Your Holy Spirit.* Ps 51:1-11. You want to petition God for help for His is the only help that fulfills your needs.

2. Sacrifice Is The Best Way To Honor God

In all ages man has found that the perfect way to offer God grateful honor, perfect thanks and his expression of sincere sorrow for sin, as well as to petition God for help was through sacrifice. Words, no matter how sincere or prayerful, were never sufficient. Man had to offer a gift to God to express adequately his inmost feelings. He felt he had to offer gifts to God. In offering sacrifice, man offers not only the gift but himself represented by the gift. Indeed a man who realizes his dependence on God, the love he owes God, his gratefulness to God, his sorrow for his sins and his Divine adoption and his need for help, wants to give himself to God.

3. Sacrifice Is The Public Offering Of A Gift To God Through A Priest

Cain and Abel, the sons of Adam and Eve, offered sacrifices (gifts) to God. Noah offered to God an animal on an altar to thank God for saving his family from the deluge. The Book of Leviticus in the Old Testament has to do with the offering of Jewish sacrifices to God.

4. Before Christ The Sacrifices Were Imperfect

The gifts, animals, grain, etc., were not perfect gifts. Then, too, the priests offering the gifts were only imperfect men. *Bulls' blood and goats' blood are useless for taking away sins, and this is what He said, on coming into the world.* Heb 10:4-5

5. Christ Gave Us The Perfect Sacrifice, The Sacrifice Of The Cross

The Eucharist is the Body and Blood of Jesus offered to God in sacrifice and the food of our souls in Holy Communion.

> At the Last Supper, on the night when He was betrayed, our Savior instituted the Eucharistic Sacrifice of His Body and Blood. He did this in order to perpetuate the Sacrifice of the Cross throughout the centuries until He should come again, and so to entrust to His beloved spouse, the Church, a memorial of His death and Resurrection: a Sacrament of love, a sign of unity, a bond of charity, a paschal banquet in which Christ is consumed, the mind is filled with grace, and a pledge of future glory is given to us. *Second Vatican Council*

At the Last Supper on the night before He died, Jesus Christ at the table with His apostles offered Himself in the perfect sacrifice. *Now as they were eating, Jesus took some bread, and when He had said the blessing He broke it and gave it to the disciples. "Take it and eat;" He said "this is My Body." Then He took a cup, and when He had returned thanks He gave it to them. "Drink all of you from this," He said "for this is My Blood, the Blood of the covenant, which is to be poured out for many for the forgiveness of sins."* Mt 26:26-28. By this act the bread and wine were changed into Christ's own Body and Blood even though the appearances of bread and wine remained. The perfect sacrifice was instituted, the priest, Christ, was perfect and the offering or gift, Christ also, was perfect.

6. Christ Gave The Apostles The Command And Power To Offer Him In Sacrifice

Christ gave the Apostles the command and the power to offer the same sacrifice when at the supper table He said: *This is*

My Body which will be given for you; do this as a memorial of Me. Lk 22:19

The apostles handed down this sacred power to the bishops and priests of the Catholic Church through Holy Orders. The offering of Christ in sacrifice is called the Mass.

7. The Mass Is The Same Sacrifice As The Sacrifice Of The Cross

In the Mass Christ offers Himself to God for all of us. In the Mass, however, although Christ is offered to God the Father, He does not suffer and die. Christ died once and for all for us.

8. St. Paul Teaches Us The Reality Of The Sacrifice Of The Mass

These words of St. Paul should make us realize once more the depth of God's love for each one of us:

> For this is what I received from the Lord, and in turn passed on to you: that on the same night that He was betrayed, the Lord Jesus took some bread, and thanked God for it and broke it, and He said, "This is My Body, which is for you; do this as a memorial of Me." In the same way He took the cup after supper, and said, "This cup is the new covenant in My Blood. Whenever you drink it, do this as a memorial of Me." Until the Lord comes, therefore, every time you eat this bread and drink this cup, you are proclaiming His death, and so anyone who eats the bread or drinks the cup of the Lord unworthily will be behaving unworthily towards the Body and Blood of the Lord. Everyone is to recollect Himself before eating this bread and drinking this cup; because a person who eats and drinks without recognizing the Body is eating and drinking to his own condemnation. 1 Co 11:23-29

9. The Mass Is The Most Perfect Act You Can Offer To God

Your own private prayers are good and important. There is, however, no act as perfect and as powerful as the offering to God of His Own Son to honor God, to thank Him, to ask forgiveness of sin and the help to continue in the Christian life.

Desire for union with the God of Salvation should lead you to the act of sacrifice which is offered to God by the Christian community at Mass. When you offer Christ at Mass actively and with your parish you gain a share in all the graces that Christ gained for us on the cross. People who are not Catholics are most welcome to offer with Catholics the Sacrifice of Mass in any Catholic Church. They may not, however, receive Holy Communion.

Mass is a public act of sacrifice to God done by a community. It is Community Worship. It is far above and far different from our private prayers, but is in no way in competition with private prayer.

10. Participate Actively In The Liturgy When You Offer Mass

The directives of the Second Vatican Council best explain how and why you should participate actively when you offer Mass.

> The Church, therefore, earnestly desires that Christ's faithful, when present at this mystery of faith, should not be there as strangers or silent spectators. On the contrary, through a proper appreciation of the rites and prayers they should participate knowingly, devoutly, and actively. They should be instructed by God's Word and be refreshed at the table of the Lord's Body; they should give thanks to God; by offering the Immaculate Victim, not only through the hands of the priest, but also with him, they should learn to offer themselves too. Through Christ the mediator, they should be drawn day by day into ever closer union with God and with each other, so that finally God may be all in all.
>
> The treasures of the Bible are to be opened up more lavishly, so that richer fare may be provided for the faithful at the table of God's Word. In this way a more representative portion of the holy Scriptures will be read to the people over a set cycle of years.
>
> By means of the homily the mysteries of the faith and the guiding principles of the Christian life are expounded from the sacred text during the course of the liturgical year. The homily, therefore, is to be highly esteemed as part of the liturgy itself; in fact, at those Masses which are celebrated with the assistance of the people on Sundays and feasts of obligation, it should not be omitted except for a serious reason.
>
> Especially on Sundays and feasts of obligation, there is to be restored, after the gospel and the homily, the common prayer or the prayer of the faithful. By this prayer, in which the people are to take part, intercession will be made for holy Church, for the civil authorities, for those oppressed by various needs, for all mankind, and for the Salvation of the entire world. *Second Vatican Council*

When people gather together at a table to eat food they are united with one another through the common meal. When the People of God gather to offer Christ and to partake of the banquet, they become united with one another through Christ their common gift offered to the Father and the common sacrificial meal of which all partake. This union of the People of God through Christ should be brought into their daily lives. *I give you a new commandment: love one another; just as I have loved you, you also must love one another. By this love you have for one another, everyone will know that you are My disciples.* Jn 13:34-35. Love of God and neighbor should be a fruit of the sacrifice and a preparation for it.

CHRISTIAN PRACTICE

Offer Jesus to God the Father with the priest and the people in your parish at least on every Sunday.

Prepare yourself for the Liturgy of the Mass by faith, penance, works of charity and by working with your parish for the apostolate of souls. Pray and sing with the congregation at Mass thus joining with the Christian community in offering Christ to God.

Try to realize that: *Every liturgical celebration, because it is an action of Christ the priest and of His Body which is the Church, is a sacred action surpassing all others.* Second Vatican Council

Think about this: *The liturgy moves the faithful filled with paschal Sacraments to be one in holiness . . . from the liturgy, therefore and especially from the Eucharist, as from a fount, grace is poured forth upon us.* Second Vatican Council

Try to understand that the liturgy especially the Liturgy of the Mass is: *the primary and indispensable source from which the faithful are to derive the true Christian spirit.* Second Vatican Council

Try to see what the Mass is: *The aim and object of apostolic works is that all who are made sons of God by faith and Baptism should come together to praise God in the midst of His Church, to take part in the Sacrifice, and to eat the Lord's supper.* Second Vatican Council

CHRISTIAN PRAYER

Offering of bread at Mass

Blessed are You, Lord, God of all creation. Through Your goodness we have this bread to offer, which earth has given and human hands have made. It will become for us the bread of life.
Blessed be God forever.

Offering of wine at Mass

Blessed are You, Lord, God of all creation. Through Your goodness we have this wine to offer, fruit of the vine and work of human hands. It will become our spiritual drink.
Blessed be God forever.

SUGGESTED READING FROM SCRIPTURE

Since they must share the abundant wealth of the Divine word with the faithful committed to them, especially in the sacred liturgy. *Second Vatican Council*

Jn 6:47-58 – Christ promised the Eucharist.
Mt 26:26-28 – The First Mass.
1 Co 14:22 – Assist at Mass reverently.
Ac 2:42-47 – The Eucharist in the early Christian community.
Ac 20:7-12 – Paul celebrated Mass with the early Christian community.

Ac 13:1-2 – The Church at Antioch offered worship.
Lk 24:13-35 – The disciples on the road to Emmaus recognized Jesus in the breaking of bread.
1 Co 11:26-32 – St. Paul warned us to prepare ourselves for the celebration of the Eucharist.
Rv 19:6-10 – The fullness of the Eucharist will be in the banquet which Christ, the Lamb of God, will celebrate with His Church in heaven.

Union With God Through His Church

Lesson 11: THE FULLNESS OF CHRIST: THE CATHOLIC CHURCH

1. The People Of God, The Church

To proclaim the Message of Salvation to all men everywhere in all time Jesus formed into one body His followers, the community of believers, the People of God. He called this body His Church.

> This was to be the new People of God. For, those who believe in Christ, who are reborn not from a perishable but from an imperishable seed through the Word of the living God, not from the flesh but from water and the Holy Spirit, are finally established as "a chosen race, a royal priesthood, a holy nation, a purchased people. . . . You who in times past were not a people, but are now the People of God." *Second Vatican Council*

2. The Shepherds In The Church, The Apostles

To proclaim the Message of Salvation, to extend His kingdom, to be present in the world for all people, to teach us, to shepherd us and to pour out His grace upon us Jesus solemnly entrusted to His twelve apostles the power, right and duty in His Church to teach, to guide and to sanctify all men. The power to teach, to guide and to sanctify was given only to the twelve apostles.

To carry on Christ's teaching the apostles were given the power and duty to teach Christ's doctrine to the world.

> Jesus came up and spoke to them. He said: "All authority in heaven and on earth has been given to Me. Go, therefore, make disciples of all the nations; baptize them in the name of the Father and of the Son and of the Holy Spirit, and teach them to observe all the commands I gave you. And know that I am with you always; yes, to the end of time." Mt 28: 18-20

The apostles were appointed by Christ to be our shepherds or spiritual rulers so that Christ through them and their successors would lead us to the kingdom of heaven. Jesus said to the apostles: *I tell you solemnly, whatever you bind on earth shall be considered bound in heaven.* Mt 18:18. Christ also said: *Anyone who listens to you listens to Me; anyone who rejects you rejects Me, and those who reject Me reject the One Who sent Me.* Lk 10:16

In many ways Christ taught the apostles His grace was to be given through them. Through the apostles Christ would forgive sins: *For those whose sins you forgive, they are forgiven.* Jn 20:23. Through the apostles Christ would give His Body and Blood to the world: *Then He took some bread, and when He had given thanks, broke it and gave it to them, saying, "This is My Body which will be given for you; do this as a memorial of Me." He did the same with the cup after supper, and said, "This cup is the new covenant in My Blood which will be poured out for you."* Lk 22:19-20

With the powers given them by Christ the Twelve were to be Christ's witnesses in the world: *You will be My witnesses not only in Jerusalem but throughout Judaea and Samaria, and indeed to the ends of the earth.* Ac 1:8

3. The Supreme Shepherd—Peter

Solemnly Jesus told Peter he was to be supreme shepherd, the head of the Church: *You are Peter and on this rock I will build My Church. And the gates of the underworld can never hold out against it. I will give you the keys of the kingdom of heaven: whatever you bind on earth shall be considered bound in heaven; whatever you loose on earth shall be considered loosed in heaven.* Mt 16:18-19

Christ gave Peter, the supreme shepherd of souls, the holy task of feeding the entire People of God His teaching and His grace:

> After the meal Jesus said to Simon Peter, "Simon son of John, do you love Me more than these others do?" He answered, "Yes Lord, You know I love You." Jesus said to him, "Feed My Lambs." A second time He said to him, "Simon son of John, do you love Me?" He replied, "Yes, Lord, You know I love You." Jesus said to him, "Look after My sheep." Then He said to him a third time, "Simon son of John, do you love Me?" Peter was upset that He asked him the third time, "Do you love Me?" and said, "Lord, You know everything; You know I love You." Jesus said to him, "Feed My sheep." Jn 21:15-17

4. Catholic Bishops And Priests Are The Successors Of The Apostles

Through consecration of bishops and the ordination of priests the powers of Jesus Christ have been handed down in the Catholic Church for nineteen hundred years. Bishops and priests of the Catholic Church are those in Christ's Body who have the authority to teach for Christ, to shepherd Christ's flock and to dispense Christ's graces to the world. Christ lives and works through His bishops and priests in His Church. He said the work of His Church was to go on even to the end of the world: *All authority in heaven and on earth has been given to Me. Go, therefore, make disciples of all nations; baptize them in the name of the Father and of the Son and of the Holy Spirit, and teach them to observe all the commands I gave you. And know that I am with you always; yes, to the end of time.* Mt 28:18-20

> It is through the faithful preaching of the gospel by the apostles and their successors—the bishops with Peter's successor at the head—through their administration of the Sacraments, and through their loving exercise of authority, that Jesus Christ wishes His people to increase under the influence of the Holy Spirit. *Second Vatican Council*

The Pope, the Bishop of Rome, is the successor of St. Peter, being supreme shepherd of the Church of Christ, having all the rights, powers and duties of Peter. The Pope is the highest Christian teaching authority in the world; he is the supreme ruler or shepherd of the Catholic Church.

While the Pope is the successor of Peter, the Catholic bishops are the successors of the other apostles. Priests share in the powers of Christ through ordination in the sacred priesthood. The Catholic priesthood has been handed down in unbroken line from Christ and the apostles in the Catholic Church for nineteen hundred years.

5. The Laity In The Catholic Church

The Church is people. The Church is not only the pope, the bishops and the priests. The Church is the members of the Church. To recall to all Christians that they, too, are members of Christ's Body and that they have a definite part to play in making the world Christian, the bishops wrote in the Second Vatican Council the following:

> In the Church, there is diversity of service but unity of purpose. Christ conferred on the apostles and their successors the duty of teaching, sanctifying, and ruling in His name and

power. But the laity, too, share in the priestly, prophetic, and royal office of Christ and therefore have their own role to play in the mission of the whole People of God in the Church and in the world.

They exercise a genuine apostolate by their activity on behalf of bringing the gospel and holiness to men, and on behalf of penetrating and perfecting the temporal sphere of things through the spirit of the gospel. In this way, their temporal activity can openly bear witness to Christ and promote the Salvation of men. Since it is proper to the layman's state in life for him to spend his days in the midst of the world and of secular transactions, he is called by God to burn with the spirit of Christ and to exercise his apostolate in the world as a kind of leaven.

The laity derive the right and duty with respect to the apostolate from their union with Christ their Head. Incorporated into Christ's Mystical Body through Baptism and strengthened by the power of the Holy Spirit through Confirmation, they are assigned to the apostolate by the Lord Himself. They are consecrated into a royal priesthood and a holy people in order that they may offer spiritual sacrifices through everything they do, and may witness to Christ throughout the world. For their part, the Sacraments, especially the most Holy Eucharist, communicate and nourish that charity which is the soul of the entire apostolate. *Second Vatican Council*

6. The New People Of God, Catholics

The new People of God, Christians, called their Church the Catholic Church. As early as the year 110 A.D. we find St. Ignatius, the Bishop of Antioch, calling the Christian family the Catholic Church: *Where Jesus Christ is, there is the Catholic Church.* In the fourth century St. Cyril, a bishop, said of the Church: *She is called Catholic, because she alone has the privilege of being known to the* whole *world, and having subjects in all parts of the world.* St. Augustine explains why the ancient Church is called the Catholic Church: *The Church is called Catholic by all her enemies, as well as by her own children. Heretics and schismatics can call the Church by no other name than Catholic: for they would not be understood, unless they use the name by which the Church is known to the whole world.*

The Catholic Church can trace its origin back to Christ and the apostles. Only the Catholic Church is endowed with all

Divinely revealed truth, all means of grace and the apostolic succession of Christ's priesthood under the chief shepherd Peter and his successors, the popes. It is only through Christ's Catholic Church, which is the all-embracing means of Salvation that we can benefit fully from the means of Salvation. *Second Vatican Council* (Modern Catholic teaching on our Protestant and Orthodox brothers is clearly presented under points 8 and 9 in this Lesson 11.)

7. Christ Is In The World In His Body, The Catholic Church

The Catholic Church is the extension of Christ, His teaching, His adoration of the Father through our liturgy, His guidance through our bishops and pastors, the successors of the apostles. Christ does through His Church all that He did when He traveled the roads of the Holy Land. He teaches, He governs us, He brings His grace to us through His Church. Christ was sent by the Father "to bring good news to the poor, to heal the contrite of heart" Lk 4:18, "to seek and to save what was lost." Lk 19:10

> Similarly, the Church encompasses with love all those who are afflicted with human weakness. Indeed, she recognizes in the poor and the suffering the likeness of her poor and suffering Founder. She does all she can to relieve their need and in them she strives to serve Christ. While Christ, "holy, innocent, undefiled" knew nothing of sin, but came to expiate only the sins of the people, the Church embracing sinners in her bosom, is at the same time holy and always in need of being purified, and incessantly pursues the path of penance and renewal. *Second Vatican Council*

Christ is so much His Church and the Church so carries on the work of Christ in the world that St. Paul calls the Church the Body of Christ. *Now you together are Christ's Body; but each of you is a different part of it.* 1 Co 12:27. St. Paul reminds us Christians: *So all of us, in union with Christ, form one Body, and as parts of it we belong to each other.* Rm 12:5. St. Paul also tells us that Christ is the Head of the Body: *Now the Church is His Body, He is its Head.* Co 1:18. Therefore, we must never think of the Church as we think of other organizations such as clubs and schools. The Church is the union in Christ of all Christians whose task is to renew the whole world. The Church is the Body of Christ. The Church is Christ in the world and you as a member of the Catholic Church share the task of bringing Christ to the whole world and the whole world to Christ.

The Church has been given various names each of which helps us to understand and love the Church better. *Christ loved the Church and sacrificed Himself for her to make her holy. He made her clean by washing her in water with a form of words, so that when He took her to Himself she would be glorious, with no speck or wrinkle or anything like that, but holy and faultless.* The Church in Scripture is called the bride of Christ, the flock of which Christ is the Shepherd, the kingdom of God, the house of God, the family of God, the temple of God, the dwelling place of God, the Holy City, the spotless lamb and our Mother.

> The Church has more often been called the edifice of God. Even the Lord likened Himself to the stone which the builders rejected, but which became the cornerstone. On this foundation the Church is built by the apostles, and from it the Church receives durability and solidity. This edifice is adorned by various names: the house of God, in which dwells His family; the household of God in the Spirit; the dwelling place of God among men; and, especially the holy temple. This temple symbolized by places of worship built out of stone, is praised by the Holy Fathers and, not without reason, is compared in the liturgy to the Holy City, the New Jerusalem. As living stones we here on earth are being built up along with this City. John contemplates this Holy City, coming down out of heaven from God when the world is made anew, and prepared like a bride adorned for her husband. The Church, that Jerusalem which is above, is also called our Mother. She is described as the spotless spouse of the spotless Lamb. She it was whom Christ loved and delivered Himself up for her that He might sanctify her, whom He unites to Himself by an unbreakable covenant, and whom He unceasingly nourishes and cherishes. Once she had been purified, He willed her to be joined unto Himself and to be subject to Him in love and fidelity. Finally He filled her with heavenly gifts for all eternity, in order that we might know the love of God and of Christ for us, a love which surpasses all knowledge. The Church on earth, while journeying in a foreign land away from her Lord, regards herself as an exile. Hence she seeks and experiences those things which are above, where Christ is seated at the right hand of God, where the life of

the Church is hidden with Christ in God until she appears in glory with her Spouse. *Second Vatican Council*

It is with joy and enthusiastic faith that Catholics in our Profession of Faith embrace our Church as they would embrace Christ.

> I profess the faith which the Catholic, Apostolic, Roman Church teaches. I believe that Church to be the one true Church, which Jesus Christ founded on earth: to which I submit with all my heart. I believe in God, the Father Almighty, Creator of heaven and earth; and in Jesus Christ, His only Son, Our Lord; Who was conceived by the Holy Spirit, born of the Virgin Mary, suffered under Pontius Pilate, was crucified, died, and was buried. He descended into hell; the third day He arose again from the dead; He ascended into heaven, sits at the right hand of God, the Father Almighty; from thence He shall come to judge the living and the dead. I believe in the Holy Spirit, the holy Catholic Church, the communion of saints, the forgiveness of sins, the resurrection of the body, and life everlasting. I believe that the Pope, the Bishop of Rome, is the Vicar of Jesus Christ on earth, that he is the supreme visible head of the whole Church, and that he teaches infallibly what we must believe and do to be saved. I also believe everything which the holy, Catholic, Apostolic, and Roman Church defines and declares we must believe. I adhere to her with all my heart, and I reject every error and schism which she condemns. *Profession of Faith in the Catholic Church*

8. Our Protestant And Orthodox Brothers

In the sixteenth century various groups called Protestants broke away from the ancient Church, the Catholic Church. Often enough men of both sides, Catholics and Protestants, were to blame for the break. We must with sorrow note that Protestants do not have the unity of government and worship which Catholics enjoy. Unlike Catholics, Protestants do not possess all the truths which God has revealed nor all the means of grace Catholics possess. *The Catholic Church has been endowed with all Divinely revealed truth and with all means of grace.* Second Vatican Council. In breaking with the Catholic Church Protestants lost the Sacrament of Holy Orders and the powers that come from the Sacrament of Holy Orders, the succession of religious powers from Christ and the apostles.

Lacking the Sacrament of Holy Orders, Protestants do not have Christ really present in Holy Communion in the Mass. Protestants do not have the Sacraments of Penance, Confirmation, Holy Orders and the Sacrament of the Anointing of the Sick. In our day sincere efforts are being made by Catholics and Protestants to bring about the reunion of Christians.

In an unfortunate dispute with the Pope in the eleventh century some Eastern Catholics broke away from the Catholic Church but retained the priesthood of Christ, thus retaining Christ really present in Holy Communion and the Mass and retaining also all the Sacraments of Christ. The main difference between the Catholic Church and the Orthodox Churches is the Papacy. The Orthodox do not recognize the Pope as the head of the Church and the representative of Christ upon earth. In our day Christ-like efforts are being made by the Bishop of Rome, Our Holy Father the Pope, and several Orthodox bishops to restore the unity that we enjoyed before the eleventh century.

9. The Effort To Restore Unity Among Christians

The modern effort to unite Christians is called Ecumenism. All Catholics are exhorted to take active part in the work of Ecumenism.

> Promoting the restoration of unity among all Christians is one of the chief concerns of the Second Sacred Ecumenical Synod of the Vatican. The Church established by Christ the Lord is, indeed, one and unique. Yet many Christian communions present themselves to men as the true heritage of Jesus Christ. To be sure, all proclaim themselves to be disciples of the Lord, but their convictions clash and their paths diverge, as though Christ Himself were divided. Without doubt, this discord openly contradicts the will of Christ, provides a stumbling block to the world, and inflicts damage on the most holy cause of proclaiming the good news to every creature. Nevertheless, the Lord of Ages wisely and patiently follows out the plan of His grace on behalf of us sinners. In recent times He has begun to bestow more generously upon divided Christians remorse over their divisions and a longing for unity. Everywhere large numbers have felt the impulse of this grace, and among our separated brethren also there increases from day to day a movement, fostered by the grace of the Holy Spirit, for the restoration of unity among all

Christians. Taking part in this movement, which is called ecumenical, are those who invoke the Triune God and confess Jesus as Lord and Savior. They join in not merely as individuals but also as members of the corporate groups in which they have heard the gospel, and which each regards as his Church and, indeed, God's. And yet, almost everyone, though in different ways, longs that there may be one visible Church of God, a Church truly universal and sent forth to the whole world that the world may be converted to the gospel and so be saved, to the glory of God. This sacred synod, therefore, gladly notes all these factors. It has already declared its teaching on the Church, and now, moved by a desire for the restoration of unity among all the followers of Christ, it wishes to set before all Catholics certain helps, pathways, and methods by which they too can respond to this Divine summons and grace. *Second Vatican Council*

While holding to our Catholic truth enunciated very clearly by the Second Vatican Council that *Christ the Lord founded one Church and one Church only* and that *it is only through Christ's Catholic Church, which is the all-embracing means of Salvation, that we can benefit fully from the means of Salvation,* Catholics must recognize the fact that *all who have been justified by faith in Baptism are members of Christ's Body, and have a right to be called Christians, and so are correctly accepted as brothers by the children of the Catholic Church.* The Catholic Church is particularly interested in establishing better relations with the Orthodox Christians because *these Churches, although separated from us, yet possess true Sacraments and above all, by apostolic succession, the priesthood and the Eucharist, whereby they are linked with us in the closest intimacy.* Second Vatican Council

Between the Catholic Church and the Protestant churches the differences are greater: *It must be admitted that in these churches (Protestant) there exist important differences from the Catholic Church, not only of a historical, sociological, psychological and cultural character, but especially in the interpretation of revealed truth,* says the Vatican Council.

With the Council it is important to note that Protestants are united to us Catholics through Baptism and that they *look to Christ as the source and center of Christian unity; they have a love and devotion to Sacred Scripture. Though we believe they have not retained the proper reality for the Eucharistic mystery in its fullness, especially because of the absence of the Sacrament of Orders, nevertheless when they commemorate His death and Resurrection in the Lord's Supper, they profess that it signifies life in communion with Christ and look forward to His coming in glory.*

The Vatican Council reminds Catholics:

> all the faithful should remember that the more effort they make to live holier lives according to the gospel, the better will they further Christian unity and put it into practice. Catholics should avoid expressions, judgments and actions which do not represent the condition of our separated brethren with truth and fairness. We should establish dialogue with Protestants.

Catholics should cooperate with Non-Catholics in efforts for the common good of humanity. We should:

> pray with other Christians, get to know the outlook of our separated brethren, be able to explain the Catholic faith to them, cooperate in social matters in a just evaluation of the dignity of the human person, the establishment of the blessings of peace, the application of gospel principles to social life, the advancement of the arts and sciences in a truly Christian spirit, and also in the use of various remedies to relieve the afflictions of our times such as famine and natural disasters, illiteracy and poverty, the housing shortage and the unequal distribution of wealth. All believers in Christ can, through this cooperation, be led to acquire a better knowledge and appreciation of one another, and so pave the way to a Christian unity. *Second Vatican Council*

The bishops of the Council *exhort the faithful to refrain from superficiality and imprudent zeal, which can hinder real progress toward unity. Their ecumenical action must be fully and sincerely Catholic, that is to say, faithful to the truth.*

Moreover, while every man has a moral obligation to seek religious truth, no one should be forced to embrace the Catholic Faith.

(In the spirit of Ecumenism and Christian brotherhood some Catholics dislike the word "Non-Catholic." Because substitute phrases are too cumbersome this author, a member of the Commission on Human Relations and Ecumenism of the Archdiocese of Chicago, has decided to continue the use of the word "Non-Catholic" until a better word is discovered.)

CHRISTIAN PRACTICE

Love the Church, people, bishops and priests as you love Christ because the Church is the Body of Christ in the world.

Work for the Church to extend its reign in the hearts of men as you would work for Christ Himself.

Give thanks to God for making us His poor and humble servants, members of His Church.

Pray to Christ, the Head, for the members of the Church.

You should love the Church as the bridegroom loves his bride.

Thank God for our union with Christ in His Church.

Practice Ecumenism according to the directives of the Second Vatican Council.

CHRISTIAN PRAYER

We come to You, Father, with praise and thanksgiving, through Jesus Christ Your Son. Through Him we ask You to accept and bless these gifts we offer You in sacrifice. We offer them for Your Holy Catholic Church, watch over it, Lord, and guide it; grant it peace and unity throughout the world. We offer them for our Pope, for our bishop, and for all who hold and teach the Catholic Faith that comes to us from the apostles. *Eucharistic Prayer at Mass*

Shower Your loving kindness upon us, Your people, O Lord; and assure us who are members of Your Church on earth a place in the heavenly Jerusalem.

Graciously receive the prayers of Your Church, we beg You, Lord; so that built upon the firm foundation of the apostles she may ever triumph over opposition and error, and serve You in safety and freedom.

Let us pray for the holy Church of God, that our Lord and God will deign to give us peace, to preserve her unity, and to guard her throughout the world, subduing principalities and powers under her sway; and that He will grant us to lead a peaceful and quiet life to the glory of God the Almighty Father. *Prayer of Good Friday*

Almighty Everlasting God, by Whose decision all things are established, mercifully regard our prayers, and in Your loving kindness preserve the Bishop chosen for us; in order that the Christian people ruled by Your authority may under this great Pontiff increase in the merits of their faith. *Prayer of Good Friday*

SUGGESTED READING FROM SCRIPTURE

The task of authentically interpreting the Word of God, whether written or handed on, has been entrusted exclusively to the living teaching office of the Church, whose authority is exercised in the name of Jesus Christ. *Second Vatican Council*

Jn 17:11; 15-17, 20, 21 – Christ's prayer for the Church.
Ep 4:11-16; 1 Co 12:27-30; Rm 12:3-8; Col 1:15-20 – The Church, the Body of Christ.
Jn 15:1-7 – In the Church Christians are united with Christ as the branches are united with a vine.
Jn 10:7-16 – We are the sheep in Christ's Church; Christ is the Shepherd.
Mt 13:44-50 – The Church, the kingdom of heaven.
1 Tm 14:15 – The Church, the house of God.
Rv 21:3 – The Church, the dwelling place of God among men.
Acts of the Apostles – The early Church.
Lk 14:15-24 – The poor, the blind, the lame and the sick are invited to be members of His Church.
Lk 1:39-55 – The Virgin Mother of God is the ideal humble member of Christ's Church.
Mt 22:1-14 – Many refused the invitation to join Christ in His Church.
Rv 19:6-9 – The loving union between Christ and His Church will be celebrated eternally in heaven.
Mk 4:26-34 – Jesus described His Church in parables as the kingdom of God.
Jn 18:33-37 – God's kingdom is an eternal kingdom not of this world.
Ep 2:13-22 – The Church is the temple of God founded by Christ.

Lesson 12: THE HOLY SPIRIT IN THE CATHOLIC CHURCH

1. The Holy Spirit Is Really God

The Holy Spirit is the Third Person of the Blessed Trinity, really God the same as the Father and the Son are really God. We should pray to the Holy Spirit as we pray to the Father and the Son.

2. The Holy Spirit Came To The Catholic Church

The Holy Spirit was sent into the Church by Jesus to take His place and to carry on His work in the Church: *but the Advocate, the Holy Spirit, Whom the Father will send in My name, will teach you everything and remind you of all I have said to you.* Jn 14:26. Fifty days after Easter we celebrate in the Church the great feast of the Holy Spirit, Pentecost Sunday. On Pentecost the Holy Spirit came to the early Church and changed the apostles from weak fearful men to the brave men of faith that Christ needed to spread His gospel to the nations:

> When Pentecost day came round, they had all met in one room, when suddenly they heard what sounded like a powerful wind from heaven, the noise of which filled the entire house in which they were sitting; and something appeared to them that seemed like tongues of fire; these separated and came to rest on the head of each of them. They were all filled with the Holy Spirit, and began to speak foreign languages as the Spirit gave them the gift of speech. Now there were devout men living in Jerusalem from every nation under heaven, and at this sound they all assembled, each one bewildered to hear these men speaking his own language. They were amazed and astonished. "Surely" they said "all these men speaking are Galileans? How does it happen that each of us hears them in his own native language? Parthians, Medes and Elamites; people from Mesopotamia, Judaea and Cappadocia, Pontus and Asia, Phrygia and Pamphylia, Egypt and the parts of Libya round Cyrene; as well as visitors from Rome – Jews and proselytes alike – Cretans and Arabs; we hear them preaching in our own language about the marvels of God." Ac 2:1-12

On Pentecost we beg our Lord to help us follow the inspirations of the Holy Spirit: *O God, on this day You have instructed the hearts of the faithful by the light of the Holy Spirit. Grant that through the same Holy Spirit we may be truly wise and always rejoice in His consolation.* The Holy Spirit is in the

Church today and comes to each Christian soul without the external signs but giving us powers beyond our natural powers.

3. The Holy Spirit Comes To Each Christian And Lives With Him

Every Christian receives the Holy Spirit in the Sacrament of Baptism and in the Sacrament of Confirmation. The Holy Spirit with the Father and the Son actually lives in the Christian: *We shall come to him and make Our home with him.* Jn 14:23

Through the Holy Spirit a Christian shares in the life of grace, God's life in his soul. The Christian is continually reminded that he is holy because the Holy Spirit dwells in him: *Didn't you realize that you were God's temple and that the Spirit of God was living among you?* 1 Co 3:16. *The proof that you are sons is that God has sent the Spirit of His Son into our hearts: the Spirit that cries, "Abba, Father", and it is this that makes you a son, you are not a slave any more; and if God has made you son, then He has made you heir.* Ga 4:6-7

4. The Work Of The Holy Spirit In Your Soul And In Your Life

The Holy Spirit enlightens your mind to accept and believe the teaching of Jesus and gives you the strength to live according to that noble belief. (See number 6 on page 105)

The gifts of the Holy Spirit are *a spirit of wisdom and insight, a spirit of counsel and power, a spirit of knowledge and of the fear of Yahweh.* Is 11:2

The fruits the Holy Spirit brings to your soul are: *love, joy, peace, patience, kindness, goodness, trustfulness, gentleness and self-control.* Ga 5:22

5. The Work Of The Holy Spirit In The Catholic Church

The Holy Spirit remains in the Catholic Church to enable her to continue the work of Christ in the world. The Holy Spirit guides the bishops and priests of the Church in their holy work of Christ – teaching His doctrine, shepherding souls and giving grace to the people.

The Holy Spirit directs all the work of Christ in the Church – the teaching of children, the care of the sick, the comforting of the sorrowful and all other works of Christ we see in the Church. For this reason the Holy Spirit is said to be the life and the very soul of the Catholic Church.

CHRISTIAN PRACTICE

Realize your dignity as a Christian raised to God's own life by the indwelling of the Holy Spirit.

Work in your neighborhood to spread the faith to others so as to make them temples of the living God.

Pray to the Holy Spirit for patience in your work.

CHRISTIAN PRAYER

Come, Holy Spirit, and from heaven direct on man the rays of Your light. Come, Father of the poor; come, Giver of God's gifts; come, Light of men's hearts. Kindly Paraclete, in Your gracious visits to man's soul You bring relief and consolation. If it is weary with toil, You bring it ease; in the heat of temptation, Your grace cools it; if sorrowful, Your words console it. Light most blessed, shine on the hearts of Your faithful—even into their darkest corners; for without Your aid man can do nothing good, and everything is sinful. Wash clean the sinful soul, rain down Your grace on the parched soul and heal the injured soul. Soften the hard heart, cherish and warm the ice-cold heart, and give direction to the wayward. Give Your seven holy gifts to Your faithful, for their trust is in You. Give them reward for their virtuous acts; give them a death that insures Salvation; give them unending bliss. Amen. *Mass of Pentecost*

SUGGESTED READING FROM SCRIPTURE

Therefore, since everything asserted by the inspired authors or sacred writers must be held to be asserted by the Holy Spirit, it follows that the books of Scripture must be acknowledged as teaching firmly, faithfully, and without error that truth which God wanted put into the sacred writings for the sake of our Salvation. *Second Vatican Council*

Jl 2:27 – The prophet Joel foretold the coming of the Holy Spirit.
Rm 8:14-17 – The Holy Spirit makes us sons of God.
Ga 5:25-26 – The Holy Spirit directs our life.
1 Co 3:16-17 – Through the Holy Spirit we are temples of God.
Ac 19:1-7 – St. Paul, by imposing hands, conferred the Holy Spirit on twelve men in the Sacrament of Confirmation.
Jn 14:16-17; 15:26; 16:13 – The Holy Spirit the spirit of truth.
Jn 14:17 – The Holy Spirit dwells in the apostles.
Jn 14:24-26 – The Holy Spirit is sent by the Father and by Jesus.
Jn 14:26 – The Holy Spirit teaches.
Jn 16:8-11 – The Holy Spirit convicts the world of sin.
Jn 14:26 – The Holy Spirit remains with us forever and reveals the true reality of Jesus.

Lesson 13: CHRIST COMES TO YOU IN THE SACRAMENTS OF THE CATHOLIC CHURCH

1. Becoming A Christian

A Christian shares in the very life of God Himself. *You will be able to share the Divine nature.* 2 P 1:4. A Christian is born again: *Unless a man is born from above he cannot see the kingdom of God.* Jn 3:3. A Christian is God's temple; God lives in him: *Didn't you realize that you were God's temple and that the Spirit of God was living among you?* 1 Co 3:16. A Christian is a son of God in all reality: *Think of the love that the Father has lavished on us by letting us be called God's children; and that is what we are.* 1 Jn 3:1

2. Christ Comes To You In Sacraments

To make you a partaker of the Divine nature, a temple of God and a son of God Christ comes to you in Sacraments. Sacraments are actions of Christ in the Catholic Church. In the Sacraments Christ gives you His grace dearly bought on the cross to have you become more and more like Him. In every Sacrament it is Christ our high priest bringing His grace to us; the priests of your parish who administer the Sacraments to the people are only the ordained representatives of Christ.

Sacraments are actions of Christ in the Catholic Church. The Sacraments are the ordinary channels of God's grace and are necessary to gain and maintain the life of grace in your soul. Protestant churches do not have all the Sacraments of Christ. The Sacraments of the Catholic Church are another way that we learn that only the Catholic Church has the fullness of Christ. In the Catholic Church we rejoice with St. John: *from His fullness we have, all of us, received — yes, grace in return for grace, since, though the Law was given through Moses, grace and truth have come through Jesus Christ.* Jn 1:16-17

3. Baptism

Baptism is a new birth, a beginning of a new life in you, the life of God brought to you by Christ. Whenever anyone baptizes it is Christ Who baptizes. Through Baptism you really become God's son: *But to all who did accept Him He gave power to become children of God.* Jn 1:11-12

4. Confirmation

After Baptism through the Sacrament of Confirmation Jesus sends the Holy Spirit once more to the Christian soul with new grace and new strength to lead the Christian life. *They who are baptized . . . are presented to the bishops . . . and by our prayers and imposition of hands they receive the Holy Spirit and are perfected with the seal of the Lord.* St. Cyprian

5. Holy Communion

Holy Communion is Jesus Christ Himself under the appearances of bread and wine uniting Himself to the Christian to nourish his soul. *I am the living bread which has come down from heaven.* Jn 6:51

6. Penance

In the Sacrament of Penance Jesus comes to forgive the sins of a baptized Christian bringing the sinner consolation and peace. *If we acknowledge our sins, then God Who is faithful and just will forgive our sins and purify us from everything that is wrong.* 1 Jn 1:9

7. Holy Orders

Through the Sacrament of Holy Orders Christ shares the work of His priesthood with other men—the bishops and priests of the Catholic Church making Himself present to offer sacrifice, to baptize, to give the Sacrament of Confirmation, to give His Body and Blood in Holy Communion, to forgive sins in the Sacrament of Penance, to anoint the sick and to bless and sanctify marriages. Through your parish priest Christ becomes for you *a compassionate and trustworthy high priest of God's religion, able to atone for human sins.* Heb 2:17

8. Matrimony

Christ stands present every time the Sacrament of Matrimony is administered to bring His grace to Christian husband

and wife, so that they can love each other as Christ loved the Church. *Husbands should love their wives just as Christ loved the Church and sacrificed Himself for her to make her holy.* Ep 5:25-28

9. The Sacrament Of The Anointing Of The Sick

In the Sacrament of the Anointing of the Sick the Christ Who *went around the whole of Galilee . . . curing all kinds of diseases and sickness among the people* comes to the Christian who is seriously ill to bring health and consolation to his soul.

10. Preparation For Receiving Sacraments

A person must prepare himself to receive a Sacrament worthily. Prayer and love of Christ are always necessary. Sorrow and commitment to Christ are required of the sinner before receiving Baptism or Penance. A sincere desire for an increase of Christ's life in our soul is necessary before receiving Confirmation, Holy Communion, Holy Orders, Marriage and the Sacrament of the Anointing of the Sick.

11. Sacraments Are Actions of Christ In His Church

Sacraments should not be looked upon as magical rites or machines of grace insuring Salvation. Sacraments are actions of Christ in His Church. They should be understood and received as actions or gestures of Christ, summoning man to friendship and union with Him.

Every Sacrament is a saving event in the life of the Church, the plan of Salvation offered by Christ in the Message of Salvation. Each Sacrament is an extension of the saving Christ where the Christian meets his Lord personally. Christ is active in each Sacrament here and now. The Sacrament not only brings the grace of Christ; it also brings the Christian face to face with Christ. *To accomplish this tremendous work Christ is always present with His Church, especially in the liturgical actions . . . He is present by His power in the Sacraments.* Mediator Dei

CHRISTIAN PRACTICE

Recollect once a day that Christ is in the world working for us in His Church and in His Sacraments.

Receive the Sacraments frequently with devotion and with a realization of your need for God's grace: *Since you have been brought back to true life with Christ, you must look for things that are in heaven, where Christ is, sitting at God's right hand. Let your thoughts be on heavenly things, not on the things that are on earth, because you have died, and now the life you have is hidden with Christ in God. But when Christ is revealed—and He is your life—you too will be revealed in all your glory with Him.* Col 3:1-4

CHRISTIAN PRAYER

O God, You make this holy night radiant with the glory of the Resurrection of our Lord. Preserve in the new members of Your family the spirit of sonship that You have conferred on them so that they may be made new in body and soul to render You singlehearted service. *Easter Vigil*

My Lord Jesus Christ, in Your blessed Sacraments You have left us memorials of Your passion and death; enable us, we pray, to adore and serve You with such faith and love so that we may always feel in our lives the effects of Your Redemption.

SUGGESTED READING FROM SCRIPTURE

In Sacred Scripture, therefore, while the truth and holiness of God always remain intact, the marvelous condescension of eternal wisdom is clearly shown, that we may learn the gentle kindness of God, which words cannot express, and how far He has gone in adapting His language with thoughtful concern for our weak human nature. *Second Vatican Council*

Ph 3:1-21 – Paul with God's grace tries to be a perfect Christian.
Jn 4:5-14 – Christ gives us His grace springing up into life everlasting.
Is 12:1-6 – Draw grace from the Savior.
Ps 112:1-0 – God lifts you up from sin.
Ga 4:1-10 – By grace Christians are sons of God, not slaves.
Ep 2:1-22 – By grace Christians are members of God.
Ps 94:1-23 – Praise to God Who gives us His grace.
Tt 3:1-8 – Only by God's grace are we different from unbelievers.

Lesson 14: CHRIST BRINGS THE LIFE OF GRACE TO YOU IN THE SACRAMENT OF BAPTISM

1. In Baptism Christ Comes To You To Give You The New Life Of The Soul

Through Baptism Christ comes to the soul that turns to Him. In Baptism Christ gives the new life, the life of grace to the soul so that the person is really born again. *I tell you most solemnly, unless a man is born from above, he cannot see the kingdom of God.* Jn 3:3-6. Baptism is the Christian washing; the word baptism means to wash. A startling fact of Baptism is that through this Sacrament Christ washes away all your sins—the effect of Adam's sin in you, all your personal sins and even the punishment you deserve for your sins.

More startling than the washing from sins in Baptism is the fact that in Baptism Christ gives you the new life of grace. He makes you a child of God. *By His own choice He made us His children.* Jm 1:18. You share in God's life: *You will be able to share in the Divine nature.* 2 P 1:4. Through Baptism Christ with the Father and Holy Spirit lives in you. *If anyone loves Me he will keep My word, and My Father will love him, and We shall come to him and make Our home with him.* Jn 14:23. Through Baptism you become "Christed" or christened, that is you belong to Christ. You become a member of His Body, the Church.

To make it possible for you to live as a Christian, Christ in Baptism gives new powers to your soul, the powers of faith, hope and love.

In Baptism Christ gives you the power of faith. With the power or virtue of faith you have the ability to believe in Christ, in His way of life and in His Church which communicates His Revelation and His grace to us. *This is why we are bold enough to approach God in complete confidence, through our faith in Him,* says St. Paul in his letter to the Christians of Ephesus.

In Baptism Christ gives us the power to hope which is the confidence that God will bring us through the trials and temptations of life to life everlasting with Him in heaven. *Bow down, then, before the power of God now, and He will raise you upon the appointed day.* 1 P 5:6

In Baptism Christ gives us the power of love or charity, the power to love God and your neighbor for the love of God: *The love of God has been poured into our hearts by the Holy Spirit which has been given us.* Rm 5:5

2. Christ Sent The Apostles Into The World To Teach All And To Baptize All

Jesus commanded the apostles: *Go, therefore, make disciples of all the nations; baptize them in the name of the Father and of the Son and of the Holy Spirit, and teach them to observe all the commands I gave you. And know that I am with you always; yes, to the end of time.* Mt 28:19-20. Without faith in Jesus and without Baptism a person cannot be saved: *He who believes and is baptized will be saved; he who does not believe will be condemned.* Mk 16:16

3. Conversion Is Necessary Before Baptism

To be worthy of Baptism a person must be sincerely sorry for his sins and commit himself to Christ Who said: *And eternal life is this: to know You, the only true God, and Jesus Christ Whom You have sent.* Jn 17:3-4. *"You must repent" Peter answered, "and every one of you must be baptized in the name of Jesus Christ for the forgiveness of your sins, and you will receive the gift of the Holy Spirit."* Ac 2:38. The principal help to beg from God while receiving instructions is conversion to Him. This is called conversion which is a turning to God and a turning away from sin. The primary reason for the religious instructions is conversion. During this course of instructions you should consult with the priest who is guiding you concerning your sins and your desire for Christ. In Baptism you will be buried with Christ in order to arise with Him. Baptism brings death to sin and life to your soul.

> We are dead to sin, so how can we continue to live in it? You have been taught that when we were baptized in Christ Jesus we were baptized in His death; in other words, when we were baptized we went into the tomb with Him and joined Him in death, so that as Christ was raised from the dead by the Father's glory, we too might live a new life. Rm 6:3-4

When you are baptized you pledge publicly before your parish that you are becoming a follower of Christ. In order to take Christ as your leader you renounce Satan and sin:

Priest:	Do you renounce Satan?
You:	I do renounce him.
Priest:	And all his works?
You:	I do renounce them.
Priest:	And all his allurements?
You:	I do renounce them.

To renounce sin and to belong to Christ means you must offer yourself to Christ and make sacrifices to remain loyal to Him: *Anyone who does not carry his cross and come after Me cannot be My disciple* Lk 14:27, says Our Lord. To renounce sin and to belong to Christ means that in Baptism you publicly profess that you will keep the commandments: *But if you wish to enter life, keep the commandments.* Mt 19:17. To renounce sin and to belong to Christ means: *You must love the Lord your God with all your heart, with all your soul, and with all your mind. This is the greatest and the first commandment. The second resembles it: You must love your neighbor as yourself.*

4. Baptism In Case Of Emergency

Because of the holiness of the Sacrament, Baptism is ordinarily given by a priest in a parish church. However, when someone is in danger of dying and a priest cannot be found, anyone can and should baptize. The person being baptized should be urged to sorrow for his sins and belief in Christ and His teachings.

5. Accepting Protestants And Other Christians Into The Catholic Church

When a Christian wishes to become a member of the Catholic Church and thus receive the fullness of Christ, he should not be baptized again if some proof of valid Baptism in another Christian church can be found. However, if proof is not available a Catholic priest will usually baptize a Christian conditionally in this manner: *If you are not baptized I baptize you in the name of the Father, and of the Son, and of the Holy Spirit.* If proof of a valid Baptism in another Christian faith is produced, the person makes a Profession of Faith in the Catholic Church.

6. Baptism Of Infants

Infants should be baptized a week or two after birth. We know for certain that a baptized infant who dies goes immediately to God in heaven. Therefore, it would be a serious fault for parents to neglect the Baptism of their own child. Although we are equally certain that a child who dies without Baptism is not punished by God in the next world, the question of his entering heaven is in doubt. It would seem, therefore, in everyday parish life that strong emphasis should be placed on the necessity of baptizing infants rather than on the unresolved question of what happens to an unbaptized child.

7. The Day Of Your Baptism

A good way to understand that new life is really given to you in Baptism is to study the manner in which the Church baptizes.

At the door of the church the priest asks,

PRIEST: What is your name? YOU: My name is

PRIEST: Do you believe in God the Father Almighty, Creator of heaven and earth? YOU: I do believe.

PRIEST: Do you believe in Jesus Christ, His only Son, our Lord, Who was born into this world and Who suffered? YOU: I do believe.

PRIEST: Do you believe also in the Holy Spirit, the holy Catholic Church, the communion of saints, the forgiveness of sins, the resurrection of the body and life everlasting? YOU: I do believe.

PRIEST: What is it that you are seeking? YOU: Baptism.

PRIEST: Do you wish to be baptized? YOU: I do.

Place your head over the font. Your sponsors touch you. The priest pours water upon your head.

PRIEST: I baptize you in the name of the Father, and of the Son, and of the Holy Spirit.

Then the priest dips his right thumb into the sacred chrism and anoints you on the crown of the head in the form of a cross.

PRIEST: May Almighty God, the Father of our Lord Jesus Christ, Who has given you a new birth by means of water and the Holy Spirit and forgiven all your sins anoint you with the Chrism of Salvation in the same Christ Jesus our Lord, so that you may have life everlasting. Amen.
PRIEST: Peace be to you. YOU: And also with you.

The priest then places upon you the white linen cloth signifying the purity and innocence of your soul now alive with God's life of grace.

PRIEST: Receive this white garment. Never let it become stained, so that, when you stand before the judgment seat of our Lord Jesus Christ, you may have life everlasting. YOU: Amen.

The priest gives you a lighted candle. Hold it in your right hand. It signifies the light of faith in your soul.

PRIEST: Receive this burning light, and keep the grace of your baptism throughout a blameless life. Observe the commandments of God. Then, when the Lord comes to the heavenly wedding feast, you will be able to meet Him with all the saints in the halls of heaven, and live forever and ever. YOU: Amen.

PRIEST: ____________, go in peace, and the Lord be with you.
YOU: Amen.

CHRISTIAN PRACTICE

Commemorate each year the day of your Baptism as your Christian birthday recalling the words of the Church on the day of your Baptism: *We beg you, Lord, graciously hear our prayers. Guard Your chosen one, ____________, with the never-failing power of the cross of Christ, with which he has been marked. Protect him so that, remaining true to the first lessons he has learned about the great glory You will confer upon him, he may, by keeping Your commandments, attain to the glory of a new birth.* Through Christ our Lord.

With your parish at the Easter Vigil Services repeat each year the promises you made at your Baptism in which you renounced forever Satan, all his works and all his allurements.

CHRISTIAN PRAYER

Almighty and Eternal God, look mercifully on the devotion of Your reborn people, who, like the hind, seek the fountain of your waters. Graciously grant that faith may sanctify body and soul through the mystery of Baptism. *Easter Vigil*

Almighty God, by the voice of Your prophets You have made known to all the members of Your Church that You Yourself are the sower of good seed and the husbandman of the chosen vine in every field of Your domain. You have made this present people Your vineyard and Your harvest. Grant them, therefore, Your strength to root out the tangle of briars and thorns, and to bring forth worthy fruit in abundance. Amen. *Easter Vigil*

SUGGESTED READING FROM SCRIPTURE

Therefore, like the Christian religion itself, all the preaching of the Church must be nourished and ruled by Sacred Scripture. *Second Vatican Council*

1 Co 12:30 – In Baptism we are brought into fellowship with Christ and His Church.
Ga 3:23-29; 4:1-11 – Baptized Christians are clothed with Christ (the white garment in Baptism).
Rm 6:1-23 – Baptized Christians are alive in Christ and dead to sin.
Col 1:9-10 – Walk worthy of your calling as a Christian.
Col 2:1-13 – Grow in the knowledge of Christ.
2 Tm 4:1-8 – Hope in Christ.
Mt 6:25-34 – Faith in Christ.
1 Jn 4:9-16 – Love of God.
Rm 8:28 – Love of God.
Jn 6:53-69 – Peter's faith in Jesus.
Ac 2:37-47 – Sorrow for sin necessary before Baptism.
Mt 3:1-6 – John the Baptist, by baptizing with water taught men to understand the Sacrament of Baptism.
Jn 1:29-34 – Much different than John's baptism of penance is Christ's Baptism with water and the Holy Spirit.
Ac 8:26-38 – Philip baptized the minister of the Queen of Ethiopia.

Lesson 15: CHRIST FORGIVES THE SINS OF CHRISTIANS IN THE SACRAMENT OF PENANCE

1. Christ's Love For Sinners

Christ hates sin and loves the sinner. Christ is a God of compassion for sinners. Christ died on the cross for sinners. *Father, into Your hands I commit My spirit.* Lk 23:46. Christ tells of the love of His Father for sinners in His story of the Prodigal Son:

> He also said, "A man had two sons. The younger said to his father, 'Father, let me have the share of the estate that would come to me.' So the father divided the property between them. A few days later, the younger son got together everything he had and left for a distant country where he squandered his money on a life of debauchery. When he had spent it all, that country experienced a severe famine, and now he began to feel the pinch, so he hired himself out to one of the local inhabitants who put him on his farm to feed the pigs. And he would willingly have filled his belly with the husks the pigs were eating but no one offered him anything. Then he came to his senses and said, 'How many of my father's paid servants have more food than they want, and here am I dying of hunger! I will leave this place and go to my father and say: "Father, I have sinned against heaven and against you; I no longer deserve to be called your son; treat me as one of your paid servants."' So he left the place and went back to his father. While he was still a long way off, his father saw him and was moved with pity. He ran to the boy, clasped him in his arms and kissed him tenderly. Then his son said, 'Father, I have sinned against heaven and against you. I no longer deserve to be called your son.' But the father said to his servants, 'Quick! Bring out the best robe and put it on him; put a ring on his finger and sandals on his feet. Bring the calf we have been fattening, and kill it; we are going to have a feast, a celebration, because this son of mine was dead and has come back to life; he was lost and is found.' And they began to celebrate." Lk 15:11-24

2. Christ Forgives Sins

To show His power to forgive sins but perhaps more to show His love for sinners Christ forgave the sins of the paralyzed man:

> Then some men appeared, carrying on a bed a paralyzed man whom they were trying to bring in and lay down in front of

> Him. But as the crowd made it impossible to find a way of getting him in, they went up on to the flat roof and lowered him and his stretcher down through the tiles into the middle of the gathering, in front of Jesus. Seeing their faith He said, "My friend, your sins are forgiven you." The scribes and the Pharisees began to think this over. "Who is this man talking blasphemy? Who can forgive sins but God alone?" But Jesus, aware of their thoughts, made them this reply, "What are these thoughts you have in your hearts? Which of these is easier: to say, Your sins are forgiven you or to say get up and walk? But to prove to you that the Son of Man has authority on earth to forgive sins,"—He said to the paralyzed man—"I order you: get up, and pick up your stretcher and go home." And immediately before their very eyes he got up, picked up what he had been lying on and went home praising God. Lk 5:18-25

Because of her faith and her love of the Master, Jesus forgave the sins of the sinful woman:

> Then He turned to the woman. "Simon," He said "you see this woman? I came into your house, and you poured no water over My feet, but she has poured out her tears over My feet and wiped them away with her hair. You gave Me no kiss, but she has been covering My feet with kisses ever since I came in. You did not anoint My head with oil, but she has anointed My feet with ointment. For this reason I tell you that her sins, her many sins, must have been forgiven her, or she would not have shown such great love. It is the man who is forgiven little who shows little love." Then He said to her, "Your sins are forgiven." Those who were with Him at table began to say to themselves, "Who is this man, that he even forgives sins?" But He said to the woman, "Your faith has saved you; go in peace." Lk 7:44-50

Because the thief on the cross asked for forgiveness Jesus forgave his sins, *"Indeed, I promise you," He replied "today you will be with Me in paradise."* Lk 23:43

3. Christ Gave The Apostles The Power To Forgive Sins

On Easter Sunday Christ gave the apostles the power to forgive sins:

> In the evening of that same day, the first day of the week, the doors were closed in the room where the disciples were, for fear of the Jews. Jesus came and stood among them. He said

> to them, "Peace be with you," and showed them His hands and His side. The disciples were filled with joy when they saw the Lord, and He said to them again, "Peace be with you. As the Father sent Me, so am I sending you." After saying this He breathed on them and said: "Receive the Holy Spirit. For those whose sins you forgive, they are forgiven; for those whose sins you retain, they are retained." Jn 20:19-23

These are the direct words of the Good Shepherd, Jesus Christ, to the first bishops of the Church. To be in His Church as the Good Shepherd, to forgive sins, to restore the life of grace to sinful Christians, Jesus gave His Church in the person of His bishops and priests the power to forgive sins. In the same words are shown Jesus' deep love and compassion for sinners.

Christ could and did forgive sins. Christ can forgive your sins no matter how serious they are because He is the Second Person of the Blessed Trinity truly God and truly man. The Christian having renounced in Baptism Satan, his works and his allurements, is not cut off forever from Christ even after he turns against Christ by committing serious sin. He can return to the Master. The most serious state of soul is that of a sinner in despair over his sins. *Though your sins are like scarlet, they shall be as white as snow; though they are red as crimson, they shall be like wool.* Is 1:18. Come to Christ in confession even though you feel unable to cope with your sins.

In the Sacrament of Penance Christ can and does forgive your sins no matter how numerous and how terrible they are as long as you are sorry and resolve, even though you are weak, not to commit the sins again. *Father, forgive them; they do not know what they are doing*, is the way Christ looks upon the sinner.

The power to forgive sins has been handed down to priests through ordination in the Catholic Church for nineteen hundred years.

4. Christ The Good Shepherd Is In The Confessional

When you go to confession in the Catholic Church you should see there not only your parish priest but Jesus Himself acting through a man. In the Sacrament of Confession (Penance) it is really Christ the Good Shepherd Who is forgiving your sins, giving to you consolation from the knowledge that the sins are forgiven and that you are once more a child of God and brother of Christ. *Peace be with you,* are the words of Christ when you kneel in sincere sorrow in the confessional. The Sacrament of Penance is primarily the Sacrament of Christ's peace; Catholics usually love the Sacrament of Confession where they know they obtain the forgiveness of Christ; there is no place for fear of the forgiving Christ.

5. Preparing To Meet The Good Shepherd In The Confessional

To prepare for confession you should remember that the Sacrament of Penance is Christ's Easter gift to you the sinner. In preparing for confession you should remember first of all Our Lord's suffering, death and Resurrection for you. Then more important than remembering each sin is a profound sorrow for all of your sins with the firm resolve not to commit them again. Go to your parish church at the hours of confessions. Prepare your soul by quiet prayer especially the Act of Contrition. Then try to remember your sins and how many times you committed each one.

6. Confessing To Christ

Go into the confessional. Kneel down and say, "Bless me Father, for I have sinned; it is .... weeks (or months) since my last confession. These are my sins." Tell your sins. Then say, "I am sorry for all of them and ask Christ to forgive me."

If you forgot anything serious it is forgiven because of your sorrow and good intention.

After leaving the confessional perform the penance the priest has given you.

A confession in which Christ can give neither His peace nor His forgiveness is one in which you either are not really sorry or one in which you have deliberately hidden a serious sin. *He who conceals his faults will not prosper, he who confesses and renounces them will find mercy.* Pr 28:13

When it is impossible to confess to a priest Christ forgives your sins when with deep love you tell Him you are sorry, provided that you go to confession later when a priest is available.

7. Abiding Sorrow For Your Sins

With David every Christian should daily admit his sins before God and try to make up for them:

> Happy the man whose fault is forgiven, whose sin is blotted out; happy the man whom Yahweh accuses of no guilt, whose spirit is incapable of deceit! . . . At last I admitted to You I had sinned; no longer concealing my guilt, I said, "I will go to Yahweh and confess my fault." And You, You have forgiven the wrong I did, have pardoned my sin. . . . Many torments await the wicked, but grace enfolds the man who trusts in Yahweh. Rejoice in Yahweh, exult, you virtuous, shout for joy, all upright hearts. Ps 32

You can make up for your past sins by fulfilling the duties of your state in life very generously and cheerfully, and by living up to the laws of God and the laws of the Catholic Church, by prayer, fasting, abstinence, by suffering the trials of life out of love for Christ, and by practicing Christian love of your neighbor.

CHRISTIAN PRACTICE

Never avoid Christ in confession because of shame for sin or disgust with your failure to avoid sin.

In the Catholic Church the season of Advent, the season just before Christmas, and Lent, the season before Easter, are special weeks of prayer and penance for sin. Try to bring the joyful spirit of Christian sorrow into your life by doing acts of prayer, penance and almsgiving for your sins and the sins of others during these two seasons of special prayer and special penance.

CHRISTIAN PRAYER

O My God, I am heartily sorry for having offended You, and I detest all my sins because I dread the loss of heaven, and the pains of hell, but most of all, because I have offended You, my God, Who are all good, and deserving of all my love. I firmly resolve, with the help of Your grace, to confess my sins, to do penance, and to amend my life.

Have mercy on me, O God, in Your goodness, in Your great tenderness wipe away my faults; wash me clean of my guilt, purify me from my sin. For I am well aware of my faults, I have my sin constantly in mind, having sinned against none other than You, having done what You regard as wrong. You are just when You pass sentence on me, blameless when You give judgment. You know I was born guilty, a sinner from the moment of conception. Yet, since You love sincerity of heart, teach me the secrets of wisdom. Purify me with hyssop until I am clean; wash me until I am whiter than snow. Instill some joy and gladness into me, let the bones You have crushed rejoice again. Hide Your face from my sins, wipe out all my guilt. God, create a clean heart in me, put into me a new and constant spirit, do not banish me from Your presence, do not deprive me of Your Holy Spirit. Be my Savior again, renew my joy, keep my spirit steady and willing; and I shall teach transgressors the way to You, and to You the sinners will return. Save me from death, God my Savior, and my tongue will acclaim Your righteousness; Lord, open my lips, and my mouth will speak out Your praise. Sacrifice gives You no pleasure, were I to offer holocaust, You would not have it. My sacrifice is this broken spirit, You will not scorn this crushed and broken heart. Show Your favor graciously to Zion, rebuild the walls of Jerusalem. Then there will be proper sacrifice to please You—holocaust and whole oblation—and young bulls to be offered on Your altar. Miserere Ps 51

SUGGESTED READING FROM SCRIPTURE

Holy Mother Church has firmly and with absolute constancy held, and continues to hold, that the four gospels just named, . . . faithfully hand on what Jesus Christ, . . . really did and taught for their eternal Salvation. *Second Vatican Council*

Lk 22:61-62 – Peter wept over his sins.
Mt 3:1-12 – John the Baptist preaches repentance for sin.

Lk 15:1-32 – John preaches God's mercy toward sinners.
Lk 13:1-9 – John preaches the necessity of penance.
Ezk 18:1-32 – The prophet Ezekiel preaches penance.
Jl 2:12-17 – The prophet Joel summons the people to penance.
Lk 4:1-8 – Jesus does penance for forty days in the desert.
Ho 14:2-10 – God reproached Israel for its sins and promised His protection and blessing if His people would ask for forgiveness.
Lk 7:36-50 – Christ forgave the sins of the penitent woman.
Mt 9:1-8 – Jesus forgave the sins of the paralytic.
Jn 20:19-23 – Jesus gave the power to forgive sins to his apostles and their successors.
Mk 2:1-12 – Jesus performed a miracle to show that He had the power to forgive sins.
Nb 14:11-20 – God forgave the sins of the Israelites.

Lesson 16: CHRIST SENDS THE HOLY SPIRIT IN THE SACRAMENT OF CONFIRMATION

1. In The Sacrament Of Confirmation, Jesus Sends The Holy Spirit To Your Soul

In the Sacrament of Confirmation the Holy Spirit comes to your soul to make you strong in Christian belief and strong in the Christian life. In Confirmation the Holy Spirit fortifies, strengthens, completes, perfects and consolidates what He did in Baptism. Baptism is birth in the life of God; Confirmation brings maturity to that life. Baptism makes you a member of Christ's family; Confirmation makes you a soldier of Christ.

2. The Apostles Administered The Sacrament Of Confirmation

Christ promised to send the Holy Spirit to the apostles and did so.

> When Pentecost day came round, they had all met in one room, when suddenly they heard what sounded like a powerful wind from heaven, the noise of which filled the entire house in which they were sitting; and something appeared to them that seemed like tongues of fire; these separated and came to rest on the head of each of them. They were all filled with the Holy Spirit, and began to speak foreign languages as the Spirit gave them the gift of speech. Ac 2:1-4

We read then in the Acts of the Apostles that the apostles brought the Holy Spirit to the people in the Sacrament of Confirmation: *When the apostles in Jerusalem heard that Samaria had accepted the Word of God, they sent Peter and John to them, and they went down there, and prayed for the Samaritans to receive the Holy Spirit, for as yet He had not come down on any of them: they had only been baptized in the name of the Lord Jesus. Then they laid hands on them, and they received the Holy Spirit.* Ac 8:14-17

St. Paul administered the Sacrament of Confirmation to the Christians at Ephesus:

> While Apollo was in Corinth, Paul made his way overland as far as Ephesus, where he found a number of disciples. When he asked, "Did you receive the Holy Spirit when you became believers?" they answered, "No, we were never even told there was such a thing as a Holy Spirit." "Then how were you baptized?" he asked. "With John's baptism" they replied. "John's

baptism" said Paul "was a baptism of repentance; but he insisted that the people should believe in the One Who was to come after him—in other words Jesus." When they heard this, they were baptized in the name of the Lord Jesus, and the moment Paul had laid hands on them the Holy Spirit came down on them, and they began to speak with tongues and to prophesy. There were about twelve of these men. Ac 19:1-7

St. Jerome in the fourth century taught the reality of the Sacrament of Confirmation: *The imposition of hands should be performed over baptized persons and the Holy Spirit thus invoked . . . were there no Scriptural authority at hand, the consent of the whole world in this regard would have the force of law.*

3. Preparation For The Sacrament Of Confirmation

The bishop, a successor to the apostles, is the one who ordinarily gives you the Sacrament of Confirmation in the Catholic Church today. In special circumstances the Church gives some priests the power to confirm.

The Sacrament of Confirmation is usually given to a Catholic who is ten or eleven years of age and to an adult convert to the Catholic Faith. It would be sinful to neglect to receive this Sacrament, especially in our age when the danger to our Christian faith and morality is so pronounced.

If possible you should prepare for the Sacrament by retreating from the world to a place of prayer for a few days or a week. To help you prepare, some instruction in the truths of the Catholic Faith is usually given by a priest of your parish.

4. The Administration Of The Sacrament Of Confirmation In Your Parish Church

Confirmation is the occasion of a big celebration in every parish church. The church is beautifully decorated and clergy from all the neighboring parishes are present to honor the bishop and the Sacrament he will give this day. The very solemnity of the occasion makes the Christian realize the new state to which he is being elevated and the obligation to spread the Faith that comes with Confirmation.

The bishop enters the church in the procession as the congregation sing a psalm or other appropriate hymn. The bishop occupies the presidential chair in the sanctuary. A lay lector proclaims an appropriate passage from Scripture. Psalms or other chants are sung by the congregation. The pastor or another priest, after receiving the bishop's blessing, reads a passage from one of the gospels. A priest gives a homily. Then the bishop leads all the Catholics who are present in a renewal of their baptismal promises.

The bishop prays that the Holy Spirit come to each of the persons being confirmed.

BISHOP: May the Holy Spirit descend upon you and the power of the Most High preserve you from sin. PEOPLE: Amen.

BISHOP: Our help is in the name of the Lord. PEOPLE: Who made heaven and earth.

BISHOP: O Lord, hear my prayer. PEOPLE: And let my cry come to you.

BISHOP: The Lord be with you. PEOPLE: And with your spirit.

BISHOP: Let us pray. Almighty and Eternal God, Who in Your kindness gave to these Your servants a new birth through water and the Holy Spirit, and granted to them remission of all their sins; send forth from heaven upon them Your Sevenfold Spirit, the Holy Consoler. PEOPLE: Amen.

BISHOP: The Spirit of wisdom and understanding. PEOPLE: Amen.

BISHOP: The Spirit of counsel and fortitude. PEOPLE: Amen.

BISHOP: The Spirit of knowledge and piety. PEOPLE: Amen.

BISHOP: Mercifully fill them with the Spirit of Your fear, and seal them with the sign of the cross of Christ, that they may obtain everlasting life. Through the same Jesus Christ, Your Son, our Lord, Who lives and reigns with You in the unity of the Holy Spirit, God, forever and ever. PEOPLE: Amen.

The bishop then administers the Sacrament of Confirmation.

BISHOP: I sign you with the sign of the cross and I confirm you with the chrism of Salvation. In the name of the Father, and of the Son, and of the Holy Spirit. PERSON: Amen.

The bishop strikes the person gently on the cheek, saying:

BISHOP: Peace be with you.

The cross imprinted on the forehead means that the new soldier of Christ carries aloft the banner of his King in the most conspicuous part of his body proclaiming to the world his desire to fight for the glory of God and the faith of Christ. The anointing with oil means that the confirmed Christian is armed with the strength of the Holy Spirit. The gentle slap on the cheek is the kiss of Christian peace given to him at Confirmation.

5. Christ Acts In The World Through The Confirmed Christian

Realize the duty placed upon you once you are confirmed. Yours is the task of bringing Christ, His example, His way of life and His Church to others.

> You are the light of the world. A city built on a hill-top cannot be hidden. No one lights a lamp to put it under a tub; they put it on the lamp-stand where it shines for everyone in the house. In the same way your light must shine in the sight of men, so that, seeing your good works, they may give the praise to your Father in heaven. Do not imagine that I have come to abolish the law or the prophets. I have come not to abolish but to complete them. I tell you solemnly, till heaven and earth disappear, not one dot, not one little stroke, shall disappear from the law until its purpose is achieved. Therefore, the man who infringes even one of the least of these commandments and teaches others to do the same will be considered the least in the kingdom of heaven; but the man who keeps them and teaches them will be considered great in the kingdom of heaven. Mt 5:14-19

In the very beginning of the Church, the work of the apostolic laymen is evident. See Ac 11:19; Ac 18:26; Rm 16:1-16; Phm 4:3.

6. The Bishops Of The Second Vatican Council Remind The Modern Layman Of Their Role In The Catholic Church

In the Second Vatican Council the bishops of the Church in their Decree on the Apostolate of the Laity bring to the minds of the laity their call to the lay apostolate:

> Wishing to intensify the apostolic activity of the People of God, this most holy Synod earnestly addresses itself to the laity, whose proper and indispensable role in the mission of the Church it has already called to mind in other documents.

The layman's apostolate derives from his Christian vocation, and the Church can never be without it. Sacred Scripture clearly shows how spontaneous and fruitful such activity was at the very beginning of the Church. Our own times require of the laity no less zeal. In fact, modern conditions demand that their apostolate be thoroughly broadened and intensified. The constant expansion of population, scientific and technical progress, and the tightening of bonds between men have not only immensely widened the field of the lay apostolate, a field which is for the most part accessible only to them. These developments have themselves raised new problems which cry out for the skillful concern and attention of the laity. This apostolate becomes more imperative in view of the fact that many areas of human life have become very largely autonomous. This is as it should be, but it sometimes involves a certain withdrawal from ethical and religious influences and a serious danger to Christian life. Besides, in many places where priests are very few or, in some instances, are deprived of due freedom in their ministry, the Church could scarcely be present and functioning without the activity of the laity. An indication of this manifold and pressing need is the unmistakable work of the Holy Spirit in making the laity today even more conscious of their own responsibility and inspiring them everywhere to serve Christ and the Church.

The layman's religious program of life should take its special quality from his status as a married man and a family man, or as one who is unmarried or widowed, from his state of health, and from his professional and social activity. He should not cease to develop earnestly the qualities and talents bestowed on him in accord with these conditions of life, and he should make use of the gifts which he has received from the Holy Spirit.

Furthermore, the laity who in pursuit of their vocation have become members of one of the associations or institutes approved by the Church are trying faithfully to adopt the special characteristics of the spiritual life which are proper to these as well. They should also hold in high esteem professional skill, family and civic spirit, and the virtues relating to social behavior, namely, honesty, justice, sincerity, kindness, and courage, without which there can be no true Christian life.

CHRISTIAN PRACTICE

Be openly fervent in the practice of your faith, give good example to your family and associates, do everything possible to bring others to the fullness of Christ which we can obtain only in the Catholic Church.

Perform the works of Christian mercy from love of Christ and a realization of the reward He will give you: *Then the King will say to those on His right hand, "Come, you whom My Father has blessed, take for your heritage the kingdom prepared for you since the foundation of the world. For I was hungry and you gave Me food; I was thirsty and you gave Me drink; I was a stranger and you made Me welcome; naked and you clothed Me, sick and you visited Me, in prison and you came to see Me." Then the virtuous will say to Him in reply, "Lord, when did we see You hungry and feed You; or thirsty and give You drink? When did we see You a stranger and make You welcome; naked and clothe You; sick or in prison and go to see You?" And the King will answer, "I tell you solemnly, in so far as you did this to one of the least of these brothers of Mine, you did it to Me."* Mt 25:34-40

CHRISTIAN PRAYER

Father, All Powerful and Ever-living God, we do well always and everywhere to give You thanks through Jesus Christ our Lord. He returned to You in glory to take His place at Your right hand. On this day, true to His promise, He sent the Holy Spirit to dwell in us and make us children of the Father. So now in boundless joy the whole wide world joins with the angels in their unending hymn of praise: Holy, Holy, Holy Lord, God of power and might, heaven and earth are full of Your glory. Hosanna in the highest. Blessed is He Who comes in the name of the Lord. Hosanna in the highest. *Mass of the Holy Spirit*

O God, on this day You have taught the hearts of the faithful by the light of the Holy Spirit. Grant that through the same Holy Spirit we may be truly wise and always rejoice in His consolation. *Mass of Pentecost*

The Spirit of the Lord fills the world, alleluia, is all-embracing, and knows man's utterance, alleluia, alleluia, alleluia. *Mass of Pentecost*

God arises; His enemies are scattered, and those who hate Him flee before Him. *Mass at Pentecost*

SUGGESTED READING FROM SCRIPTURE

All Scripture is inspired by God and useful for teaching, for reproving, for correcting, for instruction in justice. *Second Vatican Council*

- Ac 2:1-11 – The Holy Spirit confirms the apostles.
- Jn 14:23-31 – Christ's promise of the Holy Spirit.
- Ac 10:34-48 – The Holy Spirit comes to the people to whom Peter was preaching.
- Ac 8:14-17 – Peter and John give Confirmation to the people of Samaria.

Ac 5:12-16 – Signs and wonders done by the apostles through the inspiration of the Holy Spirit.
Jl 2:28-32 – The prophet Joel tells of the outpouring of the Holy Spirit upon the People of God.
Lv 26:3-12 – God's dwelling in His people.
Rm 5:1-5 – The love of God is poured forth into our hearts by the Holy Spirit.
Ep 4:1-32 – Confirmed Christians are no longer children.
Ep 5:1-33 – Live like children of light.
Ep 6:10-20 – Put on God's armor to resist the evil in the world.
Gn 11:1-9 – Without God's help the world becomes as confused as the people at Babel.
Ac 2:1-11 – The Holy Spirit came into the Church.
Ac 19:1-7 – St. Paul confirmed twelve men.

Lesson 17: THE LIVING CHRIST UNITES HIMSELF WITH YOU IN THE HOLY EUCHARIST

1. Christ Tells How He Longs To Be United With You

Christ's longing for union with you and with all believers is evident in His sermon on the Holy Eucharist in the sixth chapter of St. John's Gospel:

> I am the bread of life. Your fathers ate manna in the desert and they are dead; but this is the bread that comes down from heaven, so that a man may eat it and not die. I am the living bread which has come down from heaven. Anyone who eats this bread will live for ever; and the bread that I shall give is My Flesh, for the life of the world. I tell you most solemnly, if you do not eat the Flesh of the Son of Man and drink His Blood, you will not have life in you. Anyone who does eat My Flesh and drink My Blood has eternal life, and I shall raise him up on the last day. For My Flesh is real food and My Blood is real drink. He who eats My Flesh and drinks My Blood lives in Me and I live in him. As I, Who am sent by the living Father, Myself draw life from the Father, so whoever eats Me will draw life from Me. This is the bread come down from heaven; not like the bread our ancestors ate: they are dead, but anyone who eats this bread will live for ever. Jn 6:48-58

The Body and Blood of Christ is called the Eucharist (thanksgiving), the Lord's Supper, Holy Communion and the Blessed Sacrament.

When the Eucharist is given to a person as food for his soul it is called Sacrament of Holy Communion; when the Eucharist is offered to God in sacrifice it is called Sacrifice of the Mass.

Christ is present in the Holy Eucharist to be our sacrifice, our food, our life, our companion to strengthen and console us and to extend His Incarnation to all who eat His Flesh and drink His Blood.

Through this Sacrament Jesus by a miracle of love unites Himself with you as you unite yourself with food so that the Christian can say: *I live now not with my own life but with the life of Christ Who lives in me.* Ga 2:20. You should thank God for this Sacrament: *Let these thank Yahweh for His love, for His marvels on behalf of man; satisfying the hungry, He fills the starving with good things.* Ps 107:8-9

2. Christ Gave Us Himself In The Eucharist At The Last Supper

At the Last Supper on the night before He died Christ gave Himself to us in the Eucharist:

When the hour came He took His place at the table, and the apostles with Him. And He said to them, "I have longed to eat this passover with you before I suffer; because I tell you, I shall not eat it again until it is fulfilled, in the kingdom of God." Then, taking a cup, He gave thanks and said, "Take this and share it among you, because from now on, I tell you, I shall not drink wine until the kingdom of God comes." Then He took some bread, and when He had given thanks, broke it and gave it to them, saying, "This is My Body which will be given for you; do this as a memorial of Me." He did the same with the cup after supper, and said, "This cup is the new covenant in My Blood which will be poured out for you." Lk 22:14-20

Christ gave the apostles the command and the power to bring the Eucharist to the world when He told the apostles: *Do this as a memorial of Me.* Lk 22:19

The apostles gave Christ to the People of God in the Eucharist. St. Paul reminded the people of the reality of the Lord in Holy Communion: *The blessing-cup that we bless is a communion with the Blood of Christ, and the bread that we break is a communion with the Body of Christ.* 1 Co 10:15-17

All priests in the Catholic Church have the power to change bread and wine into Christ. In the Eucharist it is Christ Himself Who consecrates through the mouth of your parish priest as the words of consecration are said: *This is My Body. This is My Blood.* Lk 22:20. St. Ambrose reminds us:

The Body which we produce in the Sacrament is the same Body that was born of a Virgin. . . . It is the same Flesh of Jesus that was nailed to the cross and afterward laid in the tomb. . . . Before the consecration effected by heavenly words, it receives the name of bread; but after the consecration, it is called the Body of Jesus Christ. Before consecration, what is contained in the chalice is called wine; but after the consecration it is named the Blood of Jesus Christ. . . . And you yourselves answer Amen, which means: This is true.

3. In Holy Communion Christ Unites Us To Himself

By uniting you to Himself in Holy Communion Jesus gives not only grace but the Author of grace, Himself, the Second Person of the Blessed Trinity: *He who eats My Flesh and drinks My Blood lives in Me and I live in him.* Jn 6:56

Jesus Christ gives us His Body under the appearance of bread, and He gives us His Blood under the appearance of wine, in order that, by eating His Body and drinking His

Blood, we may be intimately united to both. Thus we become, so to say, Christ-bearers, that is, we bear Christ in our bodies when we receive His Body and His Blood. It is thus that according to St. Peter, we become partakers of the Divine nature. *St. Cyril of Jerusalem*

The Eucharist contains the same God the apostles adored in Galilee, the same God the Magi adored when they prostrated themselves before Him in Bethlehem.

In Holy Communion Christ gives an increase of the life of grace: *If you do not eat the Flesh of the Son of Man and drink His Blood, you will not have life in you.* Jn 6:53-54

Through Holy Communion you have Christ's promise of eternal life: *Anyone who does eat My Flesh and drink My Blood has eternal life, and I shall raise him up on the last day.* Jn 6:54-55

O God, we possess a lasting memorial of Your passion in this wondrous Sacrament. Grant that we may so venerate the mysteries of Your Body and Blood that we may always feel within ourselves the effects of Your Redemption. *Feast of Corpus Christi*

4. Prepare Yourself For Holy Communion

The best way to prepare your soul for union with Christ in Holy Communion is to offer our Lord and to offer yourself reverently, prayerfully and actively to God the Father in the Sacrifice of the Mass. Join yourself with Christ and with the congregation in the proclamation of the Word of God, with the great prayer of praise and thanksgiving (Canon of the Mass). Before giving you the Body of the Lord the priest turns to you and says: *This is the Lamb of God Who takes away the sins of the world. Happy are those who are called to His supper.* The people say: *Lord, I am not worthy to receive You, but only say the word and I shall be healed.* As the priest gives you Holy Communion he says: *The Body of Christ* and you answer, *Amen.*

As often as you participate in the Sacrifice of the Mass you should receive our Lord in Holy Communion because His Body is the fruit of the Sacrifice, and for you the way to eternal life. You must be fasting for one hour and of course free from serious sin. Small sins do not exclude you from Holy Communion. Confession is not necessary before Holy Communion unless you have a serious sin to confess.

To receive Holy Communion with a serious sin on your soul or without fasting would be a foolish and serious sin and a violation of the Body of the Lord.

> And so anyone who eats the bread or drinks the cup of the Lord unworthily will be behaving unworthily toward the Body and Blood of the Lord. Everyone is to recollect himself before eating this bread and drinking this cup; because a person who eats and drinks without recognizing the Body is eating and drinking his own condemnation. 1 Co 11:27-29

With sadness we must note here that one of the obstacles to union between Protestants and Catholics is our inability to celebrate the Eucharist together. Most Protestant bodies neither claim to have nor have the priesthood, the apostolic succession of the powers of Christ, the real presence of Christ in their Eucharist.

Those who are not yet Catholics cannot receive the Body of the Lord. Your parish priest looks forward with you to the day of your First Communion.

5. Christ's Actual Presence In Our Midst

Christ is actually present in the tabernacle of your parish church to receive you in humble adoration and quiet prayer whenever you visit Him. Some parishes have a public Holy Hour in which hymns of praise are sung to Christ Who is present in the Blessed Sacrament. Forty Hours Devotion is forty hours of prayer before the Blessed Sacrament. The devotion to Christ on the First Friday of each month is a devotion to Jesus Who asked the world to turn to His Sacred Heart. There are special days like the Feast of Corpus Christi (the Feast of the Body of Christ), on which Christ in the Blessed Sacrament is carried in procession. *Come, let us praise Yahweh joyfully, acclaiming the Rock of our safety; let us come into His presence with thanksgiving, acclaiming Him with music. For Yahweh is a great God, a greater King than all other gods; from depths of earth to mountain top everything comes under His rule; the sea belongs to Him, He made it, so does the land, He shaped this too. Come in, let us bow, prostrate ourselves, and kneel in front of Yahweh our Maker, for this is our God, and we are the people He pastures, the flock that He guides.* Ps 95:1-7

CHRISTIAN PRACTICE

Receive Holy Communion each time you participate in the Sacrifice of the Mass.

Visit Christ frequently in the Blessed Sacrament. Put aside some minutes every day for private prayer before the Blessed Sacrament in your parish church.

Attend Forty Hours Devotion, Benediction of the Blessed Sacrament, Corpus Christi Processions.

Learn the devotion of the First Fridays.

CHRISTIAN PRAYER

Let us therefore humbly reverence so great a Sacrament. Let the old types depart and give way to the new rite. Let faith provide her help where all the senses fail. To the Father and to the Son be praise, acclamation, Salvation, honor, might and blessing too. To the One Who proceeds from Them Both, be given equal praise. Amen.

Saving Victim, opening wide heaven's gate, wars and enemies press hard upon us; give us strength, bring us help. Everlasting praise be to the Lord, one and three. May He give us everlasting life in the land where dwells our Father. Amen.

O God, Who in this wonderful Sacrament left us a memorial of Your passion, grant, we implore You, that we may so venerate the sacred mysteries of Your Body and Blood as always to be conscious of the fruit of Your Redemption. You Who live and reign with God the Father in the unity of the Holy Spirit, God, forever and ever. Amen.

O Sacrament most holy, O Sacrament Divine! All praise and all thanksgiving be every moment Thine!

My Lord Jesus Christ, it is Your great love for men that keeps You day and night in this Sacrament, full of pity and love, expecting, inviting, and welcoming all who visit You. I believe that You are really present in the Sacrament of the Altar. From the depth of my nothingness, I adore You; and I thank You for the many graces You have given me, especially for the gift of Yourself in this Sacrament, for the gift of Your most holy Mother as my intercessor, and for the privilege of visiting You in this Church.

SUGGESTED READING FROM SCRIPTURE

The Church has always regarded the Scriptures together with Sacred Tradition as the supreme rule of faith, and will ever do so. *Second Vatican Council*

Jn 6:1-66 – Jesus' promise of the Eucharist.
Lk 22:7-20; Mk 14:22-25; Mt 26:26-29; 1 Co 11:23-25 – At the Last Supper Jesus gave us the Eucharist.

1 Co 11:17-34 – St. Paul to the Corinthians concerning reverence for the Eucharist.

Ac 2:42-47 – The Eucharist, the center of the early Christian community.

Ex 16:1-5 – The Blessed Sacrament foreshadowed by the manna sent to the Chosen People in the desert.

1 Co 11:12-29 – As the first People of God, the Jews, ate manna in the desert, the new People of God, Christians, eat of the Eucharist.

Ex 12:21-28 – The Jewish Passover of the Old Covenant prefigured the Eucharist of the New Covenant.

Lk 22:14-20 – Jesus fulfilled the Jewish Passover meal when He instituted the Eucharist at the Last Supper.

Lesson 18: CHRIST IS PRESENT IN EVERY CHRISTIAN MARRIAGE

1. Christ Is The Third Partner In Every Christian Marriage

Christian marriage is a lifelong, sacred union of husband and wife by which they give themselves in complete surrender to each other and to Christ. Christ is the third party in every marriage. In the Sacrament of Marriage Christ comes to man and wife to live with them, to give them His grace, to help them fulfill their rights and duties to God, to each other, and to their children in a holy manner until death.

No one can understand Christianity, Christian living and Christian Marriage unless he understands Christ and Christ's purpose in marriage.

The union of man and woman in Christian marriage is such a holy and sublime state that St. Paul compares it with the union of Christ and His Church. Like Christ's union with the Church the union of man and wife is a lifelong union in love.

> Wives should regard their husbands as they regard the Lord, since as Christ is head of the Church and saves the whole body, so is a husband the head of his wife; and as the Church submits to Christ, so should wives to their husbands, in everything. Husbands should love their wives just as Christ loved the Church and sacrificed Himself for her to make her holy. He made her clean by washing her in water and with a form of words, so that when He took her to Himself she would be glorious, with no speck or wrinkle or anything like that, but holy and faultless. In the same way, husbands must love their wives as they love their own bodies; for a man to love his wife is for him to love himself. A man never hates his own body, but he feeds it and looks after it; and that is the way Christ treats the Church, because it is His Body—and we are its living parts. For this reason, a man must leave his father and mother and be joined to his wife, and the two will become one body. This mystery has many implications; but I am saying it applies to Christ and the Church. To sum up; you too, each one of you, must love his wife as he loves himself; and let every wife respect her husband. Ep 5:21-33

2. In The Sacrament Of Marriage Christ Helps Christians To Fulfill God's Holy Purpose

A loving Father gave marriage to us.

> God created man in the image of Himself, in the image of God He created him, male and female He created them. God

blessed them, saying to them, "Be fruitful, multiply, fill the earth and conquer it. Be masters of the fish of the sea, the birds of heaven and all living animals on the earth." Gn 1:27-28

It was God Who gave Adam a wife:

Yahweh God said, "It is not good that the man should be alone. I will make him a helpmate." So from the soil Yahweh God fashioned all the wild beasts and all the birds of heaven. These He brought to the man to see what he would call them; each one was to bear the name the man would give it. The man gave names to all the cattle, all the birds of heaven and all the wild beasts. But no helpmate suitable for man was found for him. So Yahweh God made the man fall into a deep sleep. And while he slept, He took one of his ribs and enclosed it in flesh. Yahweh God built the rib He had taken from the man into a woman, and brought her to the man. The man exclaimed: "This at last is bone from my bones, and flesh from my flesh! This is to be called woman, for this was taken from man." This is why a man leaves his father and mother and joins himself to his wife, and they become one body. Gn 2:18-24

God's holy purpose in marriage is clear in His Word: *Yahweh God said, "It is not good that the man should be alone. I will make him a helpmate."* Gn 2:18. From marriage a man and his wife obtain a sweet and consoling companionship that is stronger than any other companionship in life. *This is why a man leaves his father and mother and joins himself to his wife, and they become one body.* Gn 2:24

From married love come children. Nature and Scripture teach us children are a blessing and a purpose of marriage. *Be fruitful, multiply, fill the earth.* Gn 1:28. St. John reminds us of this joy of marriage: *A woman in childbirth suffers, because her time has come; but when she has given birth to the child she forgets the suffering in her joy that a man has been born into the world.* Jn 16:21. God in His love for us gives us life from parents and the care we need as children from parents. The family is the most basic and most sacred of all societies. Our very lives come from loving parents, our character from their character, our beliefs, our thoughts, our virtues, the way we act.

Children are a great blessing in marriage. Their birth must never be regarded by Christians as a burden or a threat. Mutual self giving in marriage brings children who broaden the love of husband and wife and fulfills one of the purposes of the marriage. The size of the family can be determined by the spouses within the limits of the Christian law. The question of birth control, methods and kinds, legal and illegal, can be best explained and applied to an individual case by a priest.

3. In The Sacrament Of Marriage Christ Helps Us Fulfill God's Laws

To protect the most holy state, the people who enter into it, their happiness and the happiness of their children and even human society, God revealed basic and necessary laws for all marriages. God's rights in marriage are inalienable. The laws, binding all people, Catholic or not, are really two: A man may marry only one wife and a wife only one husband. The marriage union lasts until death.

> But from the beginning of creation God made them male and female. This is why a man must leave father and mother, and the two become one body. They are no longer two, therefore, but one body. So then, what God has united, man must not divide. Back in the house the disciples questioned Him again about this, and He said to them, "The man who divorces his wife and marries another is guilty of adultery against her. And if a woman divorces her husband and marries another she is guilty of adultery too." Mk 10:6-12

St. Paul makes clear for us the same teaching: *A married woman, for instance, has legal obligations to her husband while he is alive, but all these obligations come to an end if the husband dies. So if she gives herself to another man while her husband is still alive, she is legally an adulteress.* Rm 7:2-3

4. What God Has United Man Must Not Divide

Christ's teaching forbidding divorce and remarriage is very clear from His own words just quoted from Mk 10:6-12: *So then, what God has united, man must not divide. . . . The man who divorces his wife and marries another is guilty of adultery against her. And if a woman divorces her husband and marries another she is guilty of adultery too.* St. Paul repeating the command of His Master, preached the same fact: *A married woman, for instance, has legal obligations to her husband while he is alive, but all these obligations come to an end if the husband dies. So if she gives herself to another man while her hus-*

band is still alive, she is legally an adulteress. Rm 7:2-3. God's laws are for the common good; His law forbidding a second marriage while your partner is living is for the holiness of the married state, for the protection of the love of man and wife and for the children of their love and for their eternal reward, heaven. Not even the Pope can dissolve a valid Christian marriage. Legal decrees of civil courts such as divorce decrees simply do not dissolve valid Christian marriages. After a divorce is granted the man and wife of a valid Christian marriage remain man and wife before God. A Christian must not keep company with a person divorced from a valid marriage while the person's wife or husband remains alive.

If you have been married more than once or divorced, please seek the advice of a priest. From these instructions the prospect for the Catholic Faith should not become his own Church lawyer. There are some cases in which the Church has the power to dissolve a marriage that is not sacramental; one such instance is recorded in St. Paul: *However, if the unbelieving partner does not consent, they may separate; in these circumstances, the brother or sister is not tied.* 1 Co 7:15. In other cases we find that a former marriage which seems to be standing in the way of entrance to the Catholic Church can be set aside because it was always invalid. No matter what the outcome, please continue your instructions, participate in Mass and in the work of your parish.

5. A Wife Must Not Leave Her Husband, A Husband Must Not Send His Wife Away

On separations the Scriptures are clear: *For the married I have something to say, and this is not from me but from the Lord: a wife must not leave her husband—or if she does leave him, she must either remain unmarried or else make it up with her husband—nor must a husband send his wife away.* 1 Co 7:10-11. A separation is a violation of the married love and the marriage contract. The children are frequently the ones who suffer most from a separation; all children need the heart of the home, the mother, and the head of the home, the father.

However, for a most serious reason like adultery, chronic or habitual drunkenness, non-support, the Separation Court of the Catholic Church may grant a separation. You must not separate on your own accord. Neither is it permitted to go to an attorney to open such proceedings. After permission has been obtained from the Church to separate, you cannot keep company with anyone. In the Catholic Church because of the dangers connected with separation every effort is made to seek reconciliation before a separation is granted. Sometimes, however, a separation is the only solution.

6. Catholic Laws Concerning The Marriages of Catholics

Catholic laws are made to promote and protect sacramental marriages of Catholics.

A Catholic must be married in the presence of a priest and two witnesses. Normally a marriage of a Catholic in any other way is no marriage at all (an invalid union). By means of this law both parties are protected from the evils of modern pagan marriage practices that lead to unhappy marriages and unchristian homes. Catholics who violate this law are living in invalid marriages; they cannot receive Holy Communion, but are not excommunicated from the Church. However, today there are some cases in which bishops for serious reasons grant permission for mixed marriages to be contracted before Non-Catholic clergymen.

Marriages of people who are not Catholic among themselves outside of the Catholic Church are valid by law of the Catholic Church as long as the laws of God are observed. If a husband and wife, neither a member of the Catholic Church, observed all the laws of God when they were married, the priest will not "remarry" them when one or both become Catholic. A priest cannot "remarry" anyone.

Marriages of Catholics to persons of other religions or no faith at all are called mixed marriages. The Catholic Church dislikes such marriages because of the danger to the faith of the Catholic, the danger of divorce or separation, the difficulty of obtaining a Catholic education for the children of a mixed union, and the danger of a home without religion. For a very serious reason the bishop alone can give permission for a Catholic to marry a Non-Catholic, if the sanctity of marriage and the family, and the faith of the Catholic party are protected. After a dispensation for a mixed marriage is obtained, the Protestant pastor may be invited to the ceremony in the

Catholic Church so that Ecumenism and Christian brotherhood be promoted. Other privileges are given today too.

7. Preparation For Christian Marriage

Preparation for Christian marriage really begins in childhood in the home. In the truly Christian home children see the love, dedication and sacrifice necessary to obtain happiness and the blessings of a marriage where Christ teaches and gives His grace. There the father is a truly Christian father, the mother is a truly Christian mother, and the home is a truly Christian home. In that home even more than in the Catholic school the children learn Christian living. In the Christian home the parents lead the children to love of God and neighbor, love of the Church, Mass, Confession, Holy Communion. The difficulties of teenagers are avoided by the teaching of the Christian home. The period of "dating" is supervised by watchful parents. Their advice and counsel is sought when the child is old enough to choose a partner for marriage so that another Christian home will be founded.

If you are marrying a Catholic, it is necessary to inform your parish priest at least one month before the wedding. The priest must publicly announce this promise of marriage three Sundays. Catholics should be married at a special wedding Mass called a Nuptial Mass (though there is no law forbidding a marriage before a priest outside of Mass). If you are contemplating marriage with a Non-Catholic it is necessary to see your parish priest three or four months before the date of the marriage to learn if such a marriage is possible and to provide instructions for the Non-Catholic, if the Church permits this mixed marriage.

An excellent thing to do before marriage is to attend a Pre-Cana Conference or Retreat. Pre-Cana Conferences are conferences given by priests, doctors and married couples to prepare those contemplating marriage for the Sacrament and for the life of marriage. Retreats are days of special prayer and meditation usually made in retreat houses.

8. Joining Hands And Hearts In The Sacramental Marriage Contract

The way in which the bride and groom give themselves to

each other and to Christ in a Catholic marriage ceremony should impress you with the truths you have learned in this lesson.

The priest goes to the door of the Church. There he greets the bride and bridegroom to show the Church shares their joy. Mass is celebrated up to the gospel and the homily. In the homily the priest speaks about Christian marriage, the grace of the Sacrament and the responsibilities of the married couple.

PRIEST: My dear friends, you have come together in this Church so that the Lord may seal and strengthen your love in the presence of the Church's minister and this community. Christ abundantly blesses this love. He has already consecrated you in Baptism and now He enriches and strengthens you by a special Sacrament so that you may assume the duties of marriage in mutual and lasting fidelity. And so, in the presence of the Church, I ask you to state your intentions.

The priest then questions them:

PRIEST: ______ and ______, have you come here freely and without reservation to give yourselves to each other in marriage? GROOM: Yes. BRIDE: Yes.

PRIEST: Will you love and honor each other as man and wife for the rest of your lives? GROOM: Yes. BRIDE: Yes.

PRIEST: Will you accept children lovingly from God, and bring them up according to the law of Christ and His Church? GROOM: Yes. BRIDE: Yes.

PRIEST: Since it is your intention to enter into marriage, join your right hands, and declare your consent before God and His Church.

GROOM: I, ______, take you, ______, to be my wife. I promise to be true to you in good times and in bad, in sickness and in health. I will love you and honor you all the days of my life.

BRIDE: I, ______, take you, ______, to be my husband. I promise to be true to you in good times and in bad, in sickness and in health. I will love you and honor you all the days of my life.

PRIEST: You have declared your consent before the Church. May the Lord in His goodness strengthen your consent and fill you both with His blessings. What God has joined, men must not divide. Amen.

PRIEST: May the Lord bless these rings which you give to each other as the sign of your love and fidelity. Amen.

GROOM: ________, take this ring as a sign of my love and fidelity. In the name of the Father, and of the Son, and of the Holy Spirit.

BRIDE: ________, take this ring as a sign of my love and fidelity. In the name of the Father, and of the Son, and of the Holy Spirit.

The Mass continues.

At the offertory the bride and groom may bring the gifts to the altar.

After the Lord's prayer a beautiful new nuptial blessing is given.

In some places the bride and groom receive Communion also from the chalice.

Then the nuptial blessing is given.

PRIEST: Look with love upon this woman, Your daughter, now joined to her husband in marriage. She asks Your blessing. Give her the grace of love and peace. May she always follow the example of the holy women whose praises are sung in the Scriptures. May her husband put his trust in her and recognize that she is his equal and the heir with him to the life of grace. May he always honor her and love her as Christ loves His bride, the Church.

CHRISTIAN PRACTICE

Attend a Cana Conference with your wife or husband in order to bring yourself close together in marriage with Christ.

Married people should be one in flesh and one in mind. They should pray together, participate in Mass together, console one another, exhort and support one another. They should be united in joy and in adversity.

Try to realize that the trials and blessings of your family life are your key to heaven.

Avoid the pagan teachings of associates and friends who do not understand Christian marriage.

If you are unmarried avoid company keeping with separated or divorced persons.

CHRISTIAN PRAYER

Lord, may they both praise You when they are happy and turn to You in their sorrow. May they be glad that You help them in their work and know that You are with them in their need. May they pray to You in the community of the Church, and be Your witnesses in the world. May they reach old age in the company of their friends, and come at last to the kingdom of heaven.

Father, You have made the bond of marriage a holy mystery, a symbol of Christ's love for His Church. Hear our prayers for   and
With faith in You and in each other they pledge their love today. May their lives always bear witness to the reality of that love. We ask You this through our Lord Jesus Christ, Your Son, Who lives and reigns with You and the Holy Spirit, one God, forever and ever.

Father, All-powerful and Ever-living God, we do well always and everywhere to give You thanks. By this Sacrament Your grace unites man and woman in an unbreakable bond of love and peace. *Rite of Marriage*

SUGGESTED READING FROM SCRIPTURE

Catholic exegetes then and other students of sacred theology . . . should devote their energies . . . to an exploration and exposition of the Divine writings. *Second Vatican Council*

Gn 2:15-24 – God instituted marriage in the Garden of Eden.
Mt 19:3-9 – Christ teaches the inviolable sacredness of the marriage bond.
1 Co 7:1-7 – St. Paul gives advice to the married.
Tb 8:4-10 – The union of husband and wife is a holy union as exemplified by the marriage of Tobias and Sara.
Ep 5:21-33 – The union of Christian marriage is so sublime and mysterious that it can be compared to the love of Christ for His Bride, the Church.
Mk 10:6-12 – Christ's teaching against separation and divorce.
Rm 7:23 – St. Paul's teaching against separation and divorce.
Rm 1:21-27 – Filthy practices of pagans.
1 Co 7:3-5 – The marriage debt.
Pr 31:10-31 – The perfect wife.
Ps 128:1-4 – God gives a happy home to the devout.
Jn 2:1-11 – Christ sanctified marriage by His presence at the wedding feast of Cana.

Lesson 19: CHRIST EXTENDS HIS PRIESTLY WORK IN THE WORLD THROUGH THE SACRAMENT OF HOLY ORDERS

1. Jesus Christ Our Priest

St. Paul reminds us that Jesus is a compassionate priest of God sent to us men: *It was essential that He should in this way become completely like His brothers so that He could be a compassionate and trustworthy high priest of God's religion, able to atone for human sins.* Heb 2:17. Our high priest is one of us: *For it is not as if we had a high priest who was incapable of feeling our weaknesses with us; but we have One Who has been tempted in every way that we are, though He is without sin.* Heb 4:15. Christ the priest is the "go-between" or mediator between us and the Father: *For there is only one God, and there is only one mediator between God and mankind, Himself a man, Christ Jesus, Who sacrificed Himself as a ransom for them all.* 1 Tm 2:5-6

Through His priesthood Jesus Christ, the mediator between God and man, preached His gospel to the people, established His Church to carry on His work among men of all times and ages in history and gave His life, a sacrifice for our sins. All the work of Christ was dedicated and offered to God in the essential act of His priesthood, the offering of sacrifice. Christ offered to the Father the sacrifice of His own life on the cross, an act perpetuated in the Church by Christ the priest in the Sacrifice of the Mass.

2. Christ Gave The Apostles A Share In His Priesthood

Christ wanted His sacred priesthood to be shared by other men because His work and His authority, His teaching, His Sacrifice, and His grace were for all men of all time.

> All authority in heaven and on earth has been given to Me. Go, therefore, make disciples of all the nations; baptize them in the name of the Father and of the Son and of the Holy Spirit, and teach them to observe all the commands I gave you. And know that I am with you always; yes, to the end of time. Mt 28:18-20

Christ appointed the apostles to be His priests to carry on His work in the world. *He now went up into the hills and sum-*

moned those He wanted. So they came to Him and He appointed twelve; they were to be His companions and to be sent out to preach. Mk 3:13-14. On Holy Thursday Christ gave the apostles the power to change bread and wine into His Body and Blood at the Supper: *Do this as a memorial of Me.* Lk 23:19. After His Resurrection He gave them the power to forgive men's sins: *For those whose sins you forgive, they are forgiven; for those whose sins you retain, they are retained.* Jn 20:23. Christ gave the apostles the power to preach and baptize: *Go, therefore, make disciples of all the nations; baptize them in the name of the Father and of the Son and of the Holy Spirit.* Mt 28:19. Finally He gave the apostles all the power that God His Father had given to Him. *All authority in heaven and on earth has been given to Me.* Mt 28:18. *As the Father sent Me, so am I sending you.* Jn 20:21. Then He promised to be with the apostles forever: *And know that I am with you always; yes, to the end of time.* Mt 28:20

3. The Apostles Shared Their Priestly Powers With Other Men

Knowing that Christ's priesthood and Christ's Church were to be continued to the end of time, the apostles by ordaining priests and consecrating bishops passed on their priestly powers to others so that the work of Christ the priest would be continued in the world. *In each of these churches they appointed elders, and with prayer and fasting they commended them to the Lord in Whom they had come to believe.* Ac 14:23. St. Paul consecrated Timothy Bishop of Ephesus. Paul reminded Timothy of his consecration to the bishopric: *That is why I am reminding you now to fan into a flame the gift that God gave you when I laid my hands on you.* 2 Tm 1:6

In the Sacrament of Holy Orders a man is made a priest and receives the grace necessary to make the sacrifices required of such an apostolic life. By the imposition of the hands of the bishop a man is made a priest becoming a representative of Christ, having the priestly powers of Christ. Ordination of priests and consecration of bishops have been carried on for over 1900 years in the Catholic Church.

Unfortunately Protestant bodies do not have the Sacrament of Holy Orders.

4. The Work Of A Priest

The first work of a priest is to offer sacrifice to God for the sins of the people. Priests offer Christ in sacrifice at Mass. A priest teaches in the name of Christ, baptizes, forgives sins, gives Christ's Body and Blood in Holy Communion, anoints the sick, blesses persons and things with the blessing of Christ. The priest is the official witness for Christ and His Church at the marriages of Catholics.

Parish priests, moreover, care for the sick, seek out the sinners, instruct people in the Catholic Faith and teach the children in the parish school. Your parish priest is busy too with all the organizations of people in your parish. Besides their spiritual administration, priests are in charge of the administration of all the parish properties sometimes with and often without the assistance of lay boards.

You see Christ working every day in your parish in the persons of your parish priests. Besides this work you should remember that other priests are given to other labors of Christ. Priests labor in schools, in universities, in hospitals, in monasteries, in foreign missions as well as in parishes. The work of the priesthood is increasing and expanding because the priest is to lead all Christians to restore all things in Christ, to lift up not only fallen individuals but to dedicate and consecrate all society to God. Priests are the servants of the people.

> By sacred ordination and by the mission they receive from their bishops, priests are promoted to the service of Christ, the Teacher, the Priest, and the King. They share in His ministry of unceasingly building up the Church on earth into the People of God, the Body of Christ, and the Temple of the Holy Spirit. *Second Vatican Council*

Priests who belong to a diocese are called diocesan priests or secular priests because they work in the world. At ordination they make a promise of obedience to their bishop and are bound by a law of perfect chastity (celibacy). Diocesan priests do not take a vow of poverty but, of course, are bound to the Christian dictates of poverty or detachment from worldly goods that bind all Christians. Priests who are members of religious communities like the Jesuits, Franciscans, Carmelites and many others have vows of poverty, chastity and obedience.

5. Love And Respect For Priests

In the priest most people see Christ. *For there is only one God, and there is only one mediator between God and mankind, Himself a man, Christ Jesus, Who sacrificed Himself as a ransom for them all.* 1 Tm 2:5-6. In the priest people see the Christ Who taught the truth, Who forgave sinners, Who gave His grace, Who cured the sick. Most people know the priest is a man of God. *Every high priest has been taken out of mankind and is appointed to act for men in their relations with God.* Heb 5:1

Parents should consider it a high honor to have a boy aspire to the priesthood or the brotherhood in a religious community, or have a girl aspire to the sisterhood in a religious community of women in the Church. Boys and girls with such high ideals need your encouragement and your prayers. You will find your parish priest anxious and willing to help too.

6. The Ordination of Priests

The ordination of priests takes place at Mass after the Gospel has been proclaimed.

DEACON: Let those who are to be ordained priests come forward.

Then their names are called by the deacon, and each one answers:

CANDIDATE: I am ready and willing.

PRIEST (designated by bishop): Most Reverend Father, holy mother Church requests you to ordain our brothers here present for the office of presbyter (priest).

BISHOP: Do you know if they are worthy?

PRIEST: I testify that upon inquiry among the people of God, and upon recommendation of those concerned with their training, they have been found worthy.

BISHOP: We rely on the help of the Lord God and our Savior Jesus Christ and we choose our brothers here present for the office of presbyter.

PEOPLE: Thanks be to God.

The bishop addresses the people and the candidates on the duties of a priest.

The bishop then has the candidates declare publicly their intention to become priests, their intention to discharge faithfully the office of priest, their intention to lead holy lives, and their promise of obedience and respect to the bishop and his successors.

The candidates prostrate themselves while all others kneel for the Litany.

BISHOP: Listen to us, we pray, Lord our God, and pour out upon these servants of Yours the blessing of the Holy Spirit and the strength given to the priesthood. In Your sight we offer these men to be set apart for a sacred office. In Your unfailing generosity accept our decision, through Christ our Lord. Amen.

One by one the candidates go to the bishop and kneel before him. The bishop lays his hands on the head of each.

Next all priests present lay their hands upon each of the candidates.

With his hands extended, the bishop sings or says the prayer of consecration.

Assisting priests arrange the stoles of the newly ordained as they are worn by priests, and vest them in chasubles.

The bishop anoints with holy chrism the palms of each new priest who kneels before him.

BISHOP: The Father anointed Jesus Christ as Lord through the power of the Holy Spirit. May Jesus keep you worthy of offering sacrifice to God and sanctifying the Christian assembly.

The bishop presents the paten and chalice to each of the new priests.

BISHOP: Accept the gifts from the people to be offered to God. Be conscious of what you are doing, be as holy as the actions you perform, and model your life after the mystery of the Lord's cross.

BISHOP: Peace be with you.

PRIESTS: And with you.

CHRISTIAN PRACTICE

Assist your parish priests in their difficult work for souls.

Help your parish priests to lead those outside the Catholic Church to the fullness of Christ in the Catholic Church.

Cooperate in the work of your parish priests and apostolic groups.

Give honor to priests because they represent Christ: *Whatsoever these hands bless shall be blessed; and whatsoever they consecrate shall be consecrated and hallowed.* Liturgy of Ordination to the Priesthood

Tip your hat to the priest to honor him and the sacred powers that are his.

Work with your parish in the apostolic labors of your parish as if you are working with Christ Himself.

Pray for priests and bishops.

Assist young men who aspire to become priests.

Consider it an honor to be at the altar of sacrifice with your parish priest as a commentator, lector or server.

CHRISTIAN PRAYER

O Lord, You have made Your Son the one, eternal high priest for the glory of Your majesty and the Salvation of the human race; grant that those He has chosen to serve and administer His holy mysteries may be found faithful in fulfilling their ministry.

O God, You appointed Your Son, Jesus Christ, to be the eternal high priest, to offer gifts and sacrifices for sins; give us, Your Chosen People, we pray, a great love for His Holy Sacrifice and the grace to atone with Him for our faults.

O God, Who gave to Your servant, by his sacerdotal office, a share in the priesthood of the apostles, grant, we implore, that he may also be one of their company forever in heaven. Through Christ our Lord. *Burial of a Priest*

O Jesus, eternal priest, keep Your priests within the shelter of Your Sacred Heart, where none may touch them. Keep unstained their anointed hands, which daily touch Your Sacred Body. Keep unsullied their lips, daily purpled with Your Precious Blood. Keep pure and unworldly their hearts, sealed with the sublime mark of the priesthood. Let Your holy love surround them from the world's contagion. Bless their labors with abundant fruit, and may the souls to whom they minister be their joy and consolation here and their everlasting crown hereafter. Mary, Queen of the Clergy, pray for us: obtain for us numerous and holy priests.

SUGGESTED READING FROM SCRIPTURE

For what the apostles preached in fulfillment of the commission of Christ, afterwards they themselves and apostolic men . . . handed on to us in writing. *Second Vatican Council*

Heb 2:1-18 – Jesus our priest and Redeemer.
Heb 3:1-19 – Jesus the faithful and merciful high priest.
Heb 4:14-16 – Jesus the priest is one of us.
Heb 5:1-10 – Jesus the compassionate priest.
Heb 6:9-20 – Hope for Salvation from Jesus the priest.
Heb 8:1-13 – Jesus our priest meditates for us with God the Father.
Heb 9:11-28 – Christ the priest of all blessings.
Jn 9:35-37 – The need for priests.
Mt 10:1-42 – Jesus sent the apostles into the world to carry on His priestly ministry.
Jn 10:1-21 – The priest should be a good shepherd.
Ac 26:1-32 – Christ calls Paul to be an apostle.
Ep 3:1-21 – Paul called by God to give to the gentiles and to us knowledge of the mystery of Christ.
Col 1:1-29 – Paul called by Christ to preach Salvation.
1 Tm 4:1-16 – Paul the bishop instructs Timothy the bishop.
Heb 13:7-19 – Obey your religious leaders.
Jn 17:1-26 – The priestly prayer of Christ for the apostles and their successors in His priesthood.

Lesson 20: CHRIST COMES TO THE SICK IN THE SACRAMENT OF THE ANOINTING OF THE SICK

1. Christ's Special Love For The Sick

Christ has special love and care for all those in need in the world, for the sinner, the poor, the outcast, the sick. His special care for the sick is best manifested in His work in the Holy Land:

> He went round the whole of Galilee teaching in their synagogues, proclaiming the Good News of the kingdom and curing all kinds of diseases and sickness among the people. His fame spread throughout Syria, and those who were suffering from diseases and painful complaints of one kind or another, the possessed, epileptics, the paralyzed, were all brought to Him, and He cured them. Large crowds followed Him, coming from Galilee, the Decapolis, Jerusalem, Judaea and Transjordania. Mt 4:23-25

Luke tells how Christ cured people at Capernaum: *At sunset all those who had friends suffering from diseases of one kind or another brought them to Him, and laying His hands on each He cured them.* Lk 4:40-41. He cured the man with the withered hand:

> He moved on from there and went to their synagogue, and a man was there at the time who had a withered hand. They asked Him, "Is it against the law to cure a man on the sabbath day?" hoping for something to use against Him. But He said to them, "If any one of you here had only one sheep and if fell down a hole on the sabbath day, would he not get hold of it and lift it out? Now a man is far more important than a sheep, so it follows that it is permitted to do good on the sabbath day." Then He said to the man, "Stretch out your hand." He stretched it out and his hand was better, as sound as the other one. At this the Pharisees went out and began to plot against Him, discussing how to destroy Him. Mt 12:9-14

Jesus cured the woman with the bloody flux:

> Then from behind came a woman, who had suffered from a hemorrhage for twelve years, and she touched the fringe of His cloak, for she said to herself, "If I can only touch His cloak I shall be well again." Jesus turned round and saw her; and He said to her, "Courage, my daughter, your faith has restored you to health." And from that moment the woman was well again. Mt 9:20-22

Realizing the love of Christ for us, especially when we are in trouble, we can almost expect that He would come to us when we are sick.

2. In The Sacrament Of The Anointing Of The Sick Christ Comes To The Sick Person

The very clear words of Scripture teach us that Christ does come to the sick in the Sacrament of the Anointing of the Sick: *If one of you is ill, he should send for the elders of the Church, and they must anoint him with oil in the name of the Lord and pray over him. The prayer of faith will save the sick man and the Lord will raise him up again; and if he has committed any sins, he will be forgiven.* Jm 5:14-15

What the Sacrament of the Anointing of the Sick does for the sick one is in the Scriptural text just quoted. The Sacrament brings Salvation to the sick person: *The prayer of faith will save the sick man.* Through this Sacrament his sins will be forgiven: *If he has committed any sins, he will be forgiven.* St. Thomas Aquinas goes so far as to say that through this Sacrament Christ prepares a man for immediate entrance into heaven: *By the Sacrament of the Anointing of the Sick a man is prepared for immediate entrance into glory.* When Christ comes to you in the Sacrament of the Anointing of the Sick and you offer yourself, your life and the pains of your illness with sincere Christian resignation to Him and with deep sorrow for your sins we can hope that you will go immediately into heaven if you die.

3. The Sacrament Of The Anointing Of The Sick Is A Sacrament For The Living, Not For The Dead

This Sacrament should be recognized as a Sacrament for those who are seriously sick, rather than a Sacrament for the dying. Every Catholic over the age of seven who is seriously ill ought to receive the Holy Anointing. The Sacrament can be repeated and is often repeated for persons who get well and become seriously ill again.

Sorrow for sins is of course required to have sins forgiven in any Sacrament. Therefore, your parish priest should be called early to a sick person so that he can help the person to sincere sorrow for sins and a fruitful reception of the Sacrament of the Anointing of the Sick. To neglect to call the priest early is to neglect the sick person himself. In this Sacrament besides forgiveness of sin Christ comes with consolation for the soul often in pain and sometimes in deep fear and temptation. Sick people want any help they can get – doctors, medicine, and, of course, Christ and His Sacraments. Oil soothes pains. The Oil of the Anointing of the Sick soothes the pains of the person in sickness.

Before the Sacrament of the Anointing of the Sick the priest usually gives the sick person the Sacrament of Penance and after the Anointing gives the Body and Blood of Christ. The Last Blessing which brings with it a plenary indulgence is given at this time too. A good confession, the special Sacrament for the sick, union with Christ in Holy Communion and the plenary indulgence of the Church certainly gives us good reason to believe with St. Thomas that the soul goes immediately to heaven.

4. How The Sacrament Of The Anointing Of The Sick Is Given To The Sick Person

Perhaps the best way to understand the love and consolation poured forth by the loving Christ upon a sick Christian through this Sacrament is to follow the ceremony of anointing.

A table with blessed candles, a glass of water and spoon, a few small wads of cotton and a crucifix should be prepared in your home before the priest comes.

As the priest enters your home he gives the Christian greeting.

PRIEST: Peace to this house.

YOU REPLY: And all who dwell within.

The priest blesses the sick person and all present.

PRIEST: Sprinkle me, O Lord, with hyssop and I shall be purified; wash me, and I shall be whiter than snow.

The priest then prays for happiness, joy, charity and good health for all in the household.

If the sick person wishes to go to Confession all should leave the room while the priest gives Christ's consolation in the Sacrament of Penance.

The sick person then says the Confiteor and the priest asks God to forgive his sins.

The priest then reads a suitable passage from the Life of Christ relating to Christ's care and cure of the sick.

The Sacrament of the Anointing of the Sick is then given. The priest dips his thumb into the Holy Oil of the Sick and anoints in the form of the cross six parts of the body with which the sick one might have sinned, the eyes, ears, nose, lips, hands and feet. As he anoints he prays over each failing member.

PRIEST: May the Lord forgive you by this holy anointing and His most loving mercy whatever sins you have committed by the use of your hearing, by the use of your sense of smell, by the use of your sense of taste and the power of speech, by the use of your sense of touch, by the use of your power to walk.

The priest begs God's mercy upon the sick person and prays that God will cure his wounds, forgive his sins and drive away from him all pains of mind and body.

PRIEST: In Your mercy give him health, inward and outward, so that he may once more be able to take up his work, restored by the gift of Your mercy.

The sick one having been freed from sin by a good confession and by the Sacrament of the Anointing of the Sick is now prepared to be united with Christ his Lord. The priest asks all present to recite with him the Our Father. He then raises up the Blessed Sacrament in the sight of the sick preson as he announces,

PRIEST: This is the Lamb of God Who takes away the sins of the world. Happy are those who are called to His supper. Lord, I am not worthy to receive You but only say the word and I shall be healed.

The priest gives the sick person the Eucharist,

PRIEST: Receive, my brother, this food for your journey, the Body of our Lord Jesus Christ, that He may guard you from the wicked enemy and lead you into everlasting life.

The priest then prays to God the Father.

PRIEST: We beg of You that the most sacred Body of Your Son, our Lord, may be a lasting remedy of both body and soul for our brother who has just received it.

The priest then gives the Last Blessing which brings with it full remission of the punishment due to sin.

PRIEST: May our Lord Jesus Christ, the Son of the living God, Who gave to Peter His apostle the power to bind and to set free, in His most loving mercy receive your confession and give back to you that robe of grace which was first given to you in Baptism. And I, by the power given to me by the Apostolic See, grant you a full pardon and the remission of all your sins. In the name of the Father, and of the Son, and of the Holy Spirit.

CHRISTIAN PRACTICE

Call the priest to sick Catholics while they have the full use of their senses.

Visit the sick especially those without friends.

Look upon sickness in your own life as an opportunity to suffer the punishment due to your sins.

Consider sickness a reminder of your death; the best preparation for a holy death is life in Christ and for Christ.

Sickness should remind you of how unsatisfactory life in this world can be and make you look forward to a life of unending union with God in heaven.

It is the ordinary practice of a priest to bring the Sacraments of Confession and Holy Communion to people who are not seriously ill but who are unable to go to church. Simply tell the priest someone at home is sick.

CHRISTIAN PRAYER

O Lord God, You said through Your Apostle James: Is anyone sick among you? Let him bring in the priests of the Church, and let them pray over him, anointing him with oil in the name of the Lord. And the prayer of faith will save the sick man, and the Lord will raise him up, and if he be in sins, they shall be forgiven him. We implore You, Our Redeemer, that by the grace of the Holy Spirit You cure the illness of this sick man and heal his wounds; forgive his sins and drive away from him all pains of mind and body. In Your mercy give him health, inward and outward, so that he may once more be able to take up his work, restored by the gift of Your mercy.

We implore You, O Lord, look with kindness on Your servant, who is growing weak as his body fails. Cherish the soul which You created, so that, purified and made whole by his sufferings, he may find himself restored by Your healing.

Lord, holy Father, Almighty and Eternal God, by pouring the grace of Your blessing into the bodies of the sick, You watch with all-embracing care over Your creatures. Be present in Your kindness as we call upon Your holy name. Free Your servant from sickness, restore him his health, raise him by Your right hand, strengthen him by Your power, protect him by Your might and give him back to Your holy Church, with all that is needed for his welfare.

SUGGESTED READING FROM SCRIPTURE

This sacred Synod earnestly and specifically urges all the Christian faithful . . . to learn by frequent reading of the Divine Scriptures the excelling knowledge of Jesus Christ. *Second Vatican Council*

Mt 8:5-13 – Christ cures the son of the ruler of Capernaum.
Ps 90:1-17 – God's care of each person He created.

Ps 13:1-5 – God does not abandon any soul.
Ps 51:1-7 – Wash me and I shall be whiter than snow.
Si 38:1-14 – Conduct yourself becomingly in the Lord when sick.
1 Co 12:1-10 – St. Paul's conduct in temptation and sickness.
Jr 30:12-22 – God promised that He would cure the wounds that afflicted the Chosen People in Israel.
Mt 8:5-17 – Christ cured the sick and the possessed at Capernaum.
Mk 6:7-13 – Jesus sent His apostles to heal people just as He sends priests today to heal and comfort the sick in the Sacrament of the Anointing of the Sick.
Lk 10:25-37 – Jesus is the Good Samaritan Who heals our wounds.
Jm 5:13-16 – The priests of the Church have the healing power of Christ for us in the Sacrament of the Anointing of the Sick.

Union With God Through His Commandments

Lesson 21: THE COMMANDMENTS OF GOD

1. Our Grateful Response To God's Love

The agreement or covenant between God and His people included the Ten Commandments as an essential part of the Message of Salvation to Moses. Then God spoke all these words. He said,

> I am Yahweh your God Who brought you out of the land of Egypt, out of the house of slavery. You shall have no gods except Me. You shall not make yourself a carved image or any likeness of anything in heaven or on earth beneath or in the waters under the earth; you shall not bow down to them or serve them. For I, Yahweh your God, am a jealous God and I punish the father's fault in the sons, the grandsons, and the great-grandsons of those who hate Me; but I show kindness to thousands of those who love Me and keep My commandments. You shall not utter the name of Yahweh your God to misuse it, for Yahweh will not leave unpunished the man who utters His name to misuse it. Remember the sabbath day and keep it holy. For six days you shall labor and do all your work, but the seventh day is a sabbath for Yahweh your God. You shall do no work that day, neither you nor your son nor your daughter nor your servants, men or women, nor your animals nor the stranger who lives with you. For in six days Yahweh made the heavens and the earth and the sea and all that these hold, but on the seventh day He rested; that is why Yahweh has blessed the sabbath day and made it sacred. Honor your father and your mother so that you may have a long life in the land that Yahweh your God has given to you. You shall not kill. You shall not commit adultery. You shall not steal. You shall not bear false witness against your neighbor. You shall not covet your neighbor's house. You shall not covet your neighbor's wife, or his servant, man or woman, or his ox, or his donkey, or anything that is his. Ex 20:1-17

Like the first People of God we Christians accept the commandments as a part of our agreement with Him. As loving sons we see the commandments as our response in love to God's love for us. The commandments are our Christian surrender to God. The keeping of them is our daily prayer and our daily opportunity for union with Him. We walk joyfully in the commandments.

> For, Yahweh, visited by Your love and saving help, as You promised, I can find an answer to the insults, since I rely on

Your word. Do not deprive me of that faithful word, since my hope has always lain in Your rulings. Let me observe Your Law unfailingly for ever and ever. So, having sought Your precepts, I shall walk in all freedom. I shall proclaim Your decrees to kings without fear of disgrace. Your commandments fill me with delight, I love them deeply. I stretch out my hands to Your beloved commandments, I meditate on Your statutes. Ps 119:41-48

David in the Psalms tells that the commandments convert souls, give wisdom, rejoice hearts, enlighten the eyes, are sweeter than honey, and are more to be desired than gold and precious stones.

2. The Commandments Are God's Laws Of Love

All the Ten Commandments can be contained in two commandments of love. *You must love the Lord your God with all your heart, with all your soul, and with all your mind. This is the greatest and the first commandment. The second commandment resembles it: You must love your neighbor as yourself. On these two commandments hang the whole Law, and the Prophets also.* Mt 22:37-40. The first three commandments lead us to love God; the last seven commandments lead us to love of others (neighbors) for the love of God. We love God when we adore Him, the First Commandment; when we love His holy name, the Second Commandment; when we keep holy His day, the Third Commandment. We love our neighbor when we practice obedience, the Fourth Commandment; when we respect his life, the Fifth Commandment; when we respect his wife, the Sixth and Ninth Commandments; when we respect his property, the Seventh and Tenth Commandments.

3. The Commandments Teach Us Life In God

In this book each commandment will be presented in a positive way as the way to keep the life of grace gained in Baptism so as to enjoy that life with Christ here and in heaven. *But if you wish to enter into life, keep the commandments. He said, "Which?" "These:" Jesus replied "You must not kill. You must not commit adultery. You must not bring false witness. Honor your father and mother, and: you must love your neighbor as yourself."* Mt 19:17-19

And you must love the Lord your God with all your heart, and with all your soul, with all your mind and with all your strength. Mk 12:30

Whatever you eat, whatever you drink, whatever you do at all, do it for the glory of God. 1 Co 10:31

My children, our love is not to be just words or mere talk, but something real and active. 1 Jn 3:18

Make a habit of always walking in the presence of God.

Convert the sinner: Give kindly advice to sinners when it will be well received; pray for sinners; give good example to sinners; bring sinners to instructions.

Advise the doubtful: Help to explain the deep and necessary truths of religion to people who are doubtful about them; encourage them, (the doubtful) to bear their trials for love of God. Be kind and sympathetic to people.

Instruct the ignorant: Lead others to religious instructions; give people good books on the Catholic religion; answer doubts and difficulties about religion.

Teach catechism to children: *The learned will shine as brightly as the vault of heaven, and those who have instructed many in virtue, as bright as stars for all eternity.* Dn 12:3

Comfort the sorrowful: attend wakes and funerals; give your sympathetic understanding to your friends and companions when they are in sorrow. Sorrow is the hardest trial to bear and sometimes leads people into giving up God.

Bear wrongs patiently: Be meek and humble as Christ was. Do not seek revenge—wait until the anger of your neighbor has cooled. Be humble as Christ by being the first to mend a broken friendship, even when it was the other person's fault. Don't be sensitive: Bear wrongs as Christ did in His suffering and death for us. Forgive injuries: Forgive people who offend you. *Not seven, I tell you, but seventy-seven times.* Mt 18:22. Show your forgiveness by your words and by your actions.

Pray for the living and the dead: Say prayers for your friends, enemies, and for the dead. Offer up Mass, make the Stations of the Cross, visit the Blessed Sacrament for the benefit of others.

Feed the hungry and give drink to the thirsty: Give freely to charitable organizations, Catholic orphanages, other worthy causes, and especially the poor box in the church.

Clothe the naked: Give useful clothing to the poor; mend old garments for the poor; support societies that do this work.

Harbor the harborless: Support orphanages and homes for the aged and asylums for defectives. Adopt a child for the love of God. Help people who are homeless.

Visit the sick: Help them in their dreary hours of suffering and loneliness by giving them courage and hope, and bringing them gifts to show your love for them. Help them to pay their bills; take care of their affairs at home while they are sick.

Visit those in prison: By visiting those in prison, even if they are bad criminals, you are building up their self-respect and their hope in God and humanity.

Bury the dead: Attend wakes and funerals. Act as a pallbearer at funerals. Help to pay the expenses of burial when the family of the deceased is in difficulty. Have Masses said for the dead. Take care of cemetery plots. An act of charity to relatives and friends when they are in trouble is one of the greatest consolations in life.

CHRISTIAN PRAYER

Be good to Your servant and I shall live, I shall observe Your word. Open my eyes: I shall concentrate on the marvels of Your Law. Exile though I am on earth, do not hide Your commandments from me. My soul is overcome with an incessant longing for Your rulings. You reprove the arrogant, the accursed who stray from Your commandments. Avert their insults and contempt from me, since I respect Your decrees. Though princes put me on trial, Your servant will meditate on Your statutes, since Your decrees are my delight, Your statutes are my counsellors. Ps 119:17-24

Through Him, in Him, with Him, in the unity of the Holy Spirit, all glory and honor is Yours, Almighty Father, for ever and ever. *Canon of the Mass*

Where charity and love are, there God is. Therefore when we are together, let us take heed not to be divided in mind. Let there be an end to bitterness and quarrels, and let Christ Our God dwell in the midst of us. *Mass of Holy Thursday*

SUGGESTED READING FROM SCRIPTURE

Therefore, they should gladly put themselves in touch with the sacred text itself, whether it be through the liturgy . . . or through devotional reading, or through instructions suitable for the purpose and other aids. *Second Vatican Council*

Ex 20:1-17 – God gave Moses the Ten Commandments.
Is 45:18-26 – Yahweh is the God of all.
Jr 10:1-16 – The worship of idols is stupid and senseless, but the worship of God is true religion.
Dn 14:23-42 – Daniel was delivered from the lion's den as a reward for refusing to worship a false god.
Ac 17:16-29 – St. Paul at Athens preached the true worship of the one God and the folly of worshiping idols.
Dt 6:1-9 – God exhorts us to love Him with all our hearts, with all our souls, and with all our strength.
Mk 12:28-34 – Love of God and neighbor is the great commandment.
1 Jn 4:7-21 – God tells us that we must love God and neighbor because He has first loved us.

Lesson 22: THE ADORATION OF GOD

1. Adoration

Adoration or worship is the high honor we men give to God because God is all perfect and we depend entirely on Him. Man is also prompted to adore God because God in His high perfection has deigned to create us, to keep us in existence, to watch over us as a father watches over his children, to forgive our sins and even to make us like Himself in Divine grace. A realization of God's infinite perfection, our total dependence on Him, and His love for us almost force us to cry out: *You servants of Yahweh, praise, praise the name of Yahweh! Blessed be the name of Yahweh, henceforth and for ever! From east to west, praised be the name of Yahweh!* Ps 113:1-3. *Acclaim Yahweh, all the earth, serve Yahweh gladly, come into His presence with songs of joy! Know that He, Yahweh, is God, He made us and we belong to Him, we are His people, the flock that He pastures.* Ps 100:1-3

2. The First Commandment: I Am Yahweh Your God . . . You Shall Have No Gods Except Me

The First Commandment simply binds us to adoration the human mind craves. Man wants to honor God by praising Him, by serving Him and by offering sacrifice to Him.

You worship God by fulfilling the duties of your state in life (family life), by public adoration of God at Mass, by learning what God teaches, by prayer and sacrifice, by believing in God, hoping in Him and loving Him with all your heart, by practicing acts of love toward those God created—your neighbors. Every ordinary family duty, every prayer, every act of suffering, everything you do, may become an act of adoration of God if you offer it to God as such.

Adoration must not be outward alone; adoration must be from the heart. *True worshipers will worship the Father in spirit and truth: that is the kind of worshiper the Father wants.* Jn 4:23

As well as commanding and leading us to the adoration of God the First Commandment also warns us against any action that would lead us away from the true adoration of the living

God; neglect to learn the truths God has taught, or refusal to believe these truths once you understand them; leaving God's Church when you know it is the true Church; giving in to superstitious practices by which you show belief that certain persons or things have powers that only God has. *You must worship the Lord your God, and serve Him alone.* Mt 4:10

3. The Second Commandment: You Shall Not Utter The Name Of Yahweh Your God To Misuse It

The Second Commandment directs us to have respect for God's name. God's name is great: *Yahweh, our Lord, how great Your name throughout the earth!* Ps 8:1. God's name is holy: *So holy His name, commanding our dread.* Ps 111:9. We should praise God's name: *You servants of Yahweh, praise, praise the name of Yahweh! Blessed be the name of Yahweh, henceforth and forever! From east to west, praised be the name of Yahweh!* Ps 113:1-3

To honor not only God, the Father, Son and Holy Spirit, but His sacred name and everything connected with that name is a natural prompting of the human mind that knows and loves God.

St. Peter cured a blind man by pronouncing with reverence the name of Jesus: *In the name of Jesus Christ of Nazareth, arise and walk.* Ac 3:6. Salvation comes from even the name Jesus: *For of all the names in the world given to men, this is the only one by which we can be saved.* Ac 4:12

Every time you make the sign of the cross with reverence you honor God's name: "In the name of the Father, and of the Son, and of the Holy Spirit." When you say, "Glory be to the Father and to the Son, and to the Holy Spirit," you honor God and His name. "Praised be Jesus Christ" is a common Christian expression of love for God's Son. Ladies bow, men tip their hats when the name of God's Son is pronounced. *So that all beings in the heavens, on earth and in the underworld, should bend the knee at the name of Jesus.* Ph 2:10. Piously we pronounce the name of Jesus to ward off danger and temptations. Dying persons are asked simply to say, "Jesus" or "My Jesus mercy" to get consolation, peace and Salvation. Every time we say the Lord's Prayer we say, "Hallowed be Thy name."

The Church praises the name of God at the end of many of her liturgical prayers of the Mass: "Through Jesus Christ His Son our Lord Who lives and reigns with You in the unity of the Holy Spirit world without end" or "Through Christ our Lord." When the priest and the congregation bow during prayers at Mass it is often an expression of reverence for God's name.

To use the name of God irreverently, carelessly or flippantly is to sin against the Second Commandment. To use God's name with insolence, hate, scorn or abuse is a serious sin.

Vulgar or coarse language, though better avoided by Christians, is not sinful. Obscene jokes and stories are not necessarily sinful but are improper and sometimes can be an occasion of sin.

When we speak with reverence for our bishops, priests, religious sisters and brothers dedicated to God we honor God, His name and His presence among us. To speak irreverently about those dedicated to God is to sin against the Second Commandment. *"Do not touch My anointed ones," He said, "do not harm My prophets!"* Ps 105:15. Holy things dedicated to God, the Bible, the altar in your church, rosaries, holy pictures should be treated with respect.

A person honors God when in an oath he calls upon Him to witness the truth of his statement. Oaths are taken in serious matters such as a case in law: "I do solemnly swear to tell the truth, the whole truth and nothing but the truth, so help me God." To lie under oath is a serious crime. To swear an oath lightly or without sufficient reason is sinful.

> I say this to you: do not swear at all, either by heaven, since that is God's throne; or by the earth, since that is His footstool; or by Jerusalem, since that is the city of the great King. Do not swear by your own head either, since you cannot turn a single hair white or black. All you need say is Yes if you mean yes, No if you mean no; anything more than this comes from the evil one. Mt 5:34-37

When you make a vow you honor God and bind your weak will to follow Him more closely. Vows of poverty, chastity and obedience are made by priests, sisters and brothers in religious orders or congregations in the Catholic Church. Never make a vow without long, prayerful consideration and the counsel of a priest. *If you make a vow to God, discharge it without delay, for God has no love for fools. Discharge your vow. Better a vow unmade than made and not discharged.* Qo 5:34. For most serious reasons the Church acting with Christ's powers can dispense a person from the obligation of a vow.

4. The Third Commandment: Remember The Sabbath Day and Keep It Holy

For Christians the Lord's Day, Sunday, is a day of special worship of God.

> Remember the sabbath day and keep it holy. For six days you shall labor and do all your work, but the seventh day is a sabbath for Yahweh your God. You shall do no work on that day, neither you nor your son nor your daughter nor your servants, men or women, nor your animals nor the stranger who lives with you. For in six days Yahweh made the heavens and the earth and the sea and all that these hold, but on the seventh day He rested; that is why Yahweh has blessed the sabbath day and made it sacred. Ex 20:8-11

On this day prompted by sincere motives of love and adoration, we celebrate the Eucharist as a community. We hear God's Message of Salvation; we offer His Son to Him; we offer ourselves to God and we receive His Son in Holy Communion. We abstain from bodily labor in order to give ourselves, our thoughts and our actions more completely to God than we did on the other days of the week. A Christian should use Sunday for periods of prayer, for reading spiritual books and for works of charity toward his neighbors.

We hope you will celebrate the Eucharist on Sundays and Holy Days more from conviction born of love and devotion than from force of law. However, law is necessary to assist our weak wills to go to God in public adoration. Following the Third Commandment the Church binds us to participate in Mass on Sundays and Holy Days. A substantial omission of this obligation is a serious sin. To be late for Mass without reason is usually a less serious sin. In some places the opportunity and obligation of Sunday Mass can be fulfilled on Saturday evening.

With the same force of the Sunday law the Catholic Church asks all Catholics to participate in Mass on six Holy Days of Obligation. The Holy Days of Obligation in our country are Christmas Day, New Year's Day, Ascension Thursday (the fortieth day after Easter), The Assumption of the Blessed Virgin Mary (August 15), All Saints Day (November 1), the Feast of the Immaculate Conception of Mary (December 8).

A person naturally is excused from the obligation of participating in the Eucharist because of sickness, care of the sick, long distance to the Catholic Church, necessary work during the hours Mass is celebrated. Catholics well trained in the adoration of God usually do not find insufficient and foolish reasons for omitting worship.

Parents can sin seriously by encouraging or permitting their children to omit Mass on a Sunday or Holy Day of Obligation for a foolish reason. To tolerate absence from worship is to remove the foundation of Christian worship and practice.

Christians abstain from bodily labor on Sunday to obtain time to dedicate themselves to God and to give mind and body a rest. You must refrain from all unnecessary bodily (manual) labor on Sundays and Holy Days of Obligation. Manual work that is necessary is not forbidden on Sunday. Mental labor such as study is not forbidden.

Any recreation that is not sinful on weekdays is not sinful on Sunday, if it does not interefere with the obligation of attending Mass. Especially on Sunday, Christians, bearers of God's life and temples of the Holy Spirit, busy all week, should not find time for sin.

CHRISTIAN PRACTICE

Be on time for Mass and offer Mass with your parish community every Sunday and Holy Day of Obligation in a spirit of adoration, love and thanks to God, Who has given us all good things.

Provide for the religious education of your own children and help your parish to instruct children in the ways of God through the program of the Confraternity of Christian Doctrine.

Do not purchase in stores open for business on the Lord's Day.

Honor God and His holy name with small prayers even while you are busy. "My Lord and My God." "Jesus help me." "I love You, Jesus."

Always speak with reverence about God and people dedicated to Him in religious profession.

Honor God and His Son by daily prayer to Mary.

CHRISTIAN PRAYER

Who are You, O Lord, and who am I? You are infinitely great, and I am infinitely insignificant. You are the Creator of the universe, and, I am a miserable creature. You are everything, and I am nothing. In a word, You are He Who is, and I am he who is not. Thus, You being what You are, and I what I am, how can I venture to appear in Your Divine presence? *St. Francis of Assisi*

Come in, let us bow, prostrate ourselves, and kneel in front of Yahweh our Maker, for this is our God, and we are the people He pastures, the flock that He guides. Ps 95:6-7

Give thanks to the Lord, invoke His name; proclaim how exalted is His name.

For Your name's sake, O Lord, You will pardon my guilt great as it is.

Sing to the Lord and bless His name; announce His Salvation, day after day.

O God, Who wondrously re-created the universe by the blessed Resurrection of Your Son on the first day of the week, grant that we, Your people, may obtain a fuller participation in His victory by a more complete observance of the Christian sabbath.

SUGGESTED READING FROM SCRIPTURE

And let them remember that prayer should accompany the reading of Sacred Scripture, so that God and man may talk together; for we speak to Him when we pray; we hear Him when we read the Divine sayings. *Second Vatican Council*

Ac 3:1-26 – Peter cured a blind man by calling on the name of Jesus.
Ac 17:22-31 – St. Paul at Athens preached the true worship of the one true God.

Ps 14:1-7 – The foolishness of men without God.
Mt 26:69-75 – Peter wept bitterly for swearing that he did not know Jesus.
Gn 2:2-3 – After six days of creation God blessed the seventh day by resting from work.
Dt 5:12-15 – The sabbath was the day above all on which the Israelites were to rest and recall their redemption from Egypt.
Mk 2:23-28 – Jesus is Lord of the sabbath.
Mt 28:1-10 – Our sabbath, the first day of the week, was made holy once and for all time by the Resurrection of Jesus from the dead.
Mt 12:1-14 – Works of God on the sabbath.
Mt 21:12-16 – Reverence for the house of God.

Lesson 23: AUTHORITY AND OBEDIENCE

1. Authority Is From God

Authority is the right, power and duty to govern the members of a family, the members of the Church or the citizens of a country. All authority comes from God: The authority of parents is from God. *Children, be obedient to your parents in the Lord—that is your duty. The first commandment that has a promise attached to it is: Honor your father and mother, and the promise is: and you will prosper and have a long life in the land.* Ep 6:1-3. Even the authority of the government comes from God. *You must obey the governing authorities. Since all government comes from God, the civil authorities were appointed by God, and so anyone who resists authority is rebelling against God's decision.* Rm 13:1

Pope Leo XIII explains the necessity of authority:

> Every human community must necessarily have over it someone in authority; for without a head and a directing authority it would fall to pieces. Moreover it could not attain the purpose for which it came into being or was founded.

Authority comes from God for the well being of those who are subject to authority, not for the honor or gain of those exercising the right and duty of governing. Christians possessing authority should consider themselves the servants of those they govern:

> You know that among the pagans the rulers lord it over them, and their great men make their authority felt. This is not to happen among you. No; anyone who wants to be great among you must be your servant, and anyone who wants to be first among you must be your slave, just as the Son of Man came not to be served but to serve, and to give His life as a ransom for many. Mt 20:25-28

2. The Fourth Commandment: Honor Your Father And Your Mother

God brings children into the world through their parents. Then in His loving providence for the human race, He places the children under the authority of their parents until the children are able to take care of themselves. Therefore, God's order of things commands children to love, obey and respect their parents. In fact without this love, obedience and respect parents cannot fulfill their duties as parents. Without the

Fourth Commandment the family will become completely disorganized; it will be in total disorder. Besides the voice of nature and the voice of God, there is a voice of gratitude which tells us that you must love, respect, and obey your parents. Why should you be grateful? You owe your very life to your parents. And you owe the preservation of that life to your parents. *With all your heart honor your father, never forget the birth pangs of your mother. Remember that you owe your birth to them; how can you repay them for what they have done for you?* Si 7:27-28. And don't forget your father's care for you. During the best years of his life he had to support you and provide for your welfare. He had to supply food, shelter, clothing, education. This was his whole life. Parents give their lives for their children. The least children can do is give their parents love, respect and obedience.

The Holy Family of Nazareth, Jesus, Mary and Joseph, is the model for all Christian families.

> When the God of mercy determined to bring about the long-awaited work of mankind's renewal, He so arranged the basis and order of this work that its early beginnings would display to the world the wonderful image of a Divinely constituted Family. All men could then look upon this Family as the definitive model of domestic society, holiness and virtue. The Family at Nazareth was such a one. There, before shining forth on all peoples in the fullness of His light, the Sun of Justice was sequestered, that is, Christ our God and Savior, along with His Virgin Mother and that most holy man Joseph, who exercised a father's responsibility toward Jesus. We can be sure that the Holy Family exemplified in the highest degree those praise-worthy qualities of ordinary home life which spring from the mutual exercise of charity, from holiness of character and from the expression of filial devotion. For the Holy Family was to be a pattern of virtue for others. And so by Providence's kindly care such a Family came into existence. Now all Christians, of whatever condition or country, can by reflecting on this Family readily find both source and stimulus for practicing every virtue. Pope Leo XIII

This book is written for adults. It is adults who train children to love and obedience for all in authority and to the demands of the Fourth Commandment.

From sincere love of God and love of their own parents rather than from the force of the Fourth Commandment children should show their parents honor, love, respect and obedience. Honor, love, respect and obedience are the child's way to God and his opportunity to return thanks to the God of Salvation.

Children honor their parents by loving their parents, by respecting them as the true representatives of Almighty God and by obeying their lawful commands.

Children show their love for their parents by being grateful for parental love and care, by giving them signs of affection in thought and word and deed, by helping them whenever possible, by praying for them, and by contributing to the joy and peace of the entire home.

Children show respect for their parents by excusing their faults when possible, by seeking their advice, by confiding in them, and by accepting their corrections.

From love of God and love of parents children should not only obey their parents but should show a willing spirit of obedience. Children can show a willingness to obey their parents by trying to understand their parents' desires, and obeying without delay and without complaint. Children must be trained by their parents in the spirit of obedience.

Children fail in love toward their parents by hating them, by insulting them, or by treating them with contempt.

Children show disrespect toward their parents by being ashamed of them, by making fun of them or of their bad manners, by showing anger or feelings of dislike, by threatening them, by being disagreeable, by provoking them to anger, by striking them, by sulking, and by revealing the sins and faults of their parents to others.

Children sin against the obedience they owe their parents by refusing to follow their lawful commands. Children are obliged to obey parents in all that is not sinful.

Older children are not obliged to obey their parents in choosing a partner for marriage or in choosing to become a priest, sister or religious brother. Children should, however, consult with their parents on their choice of a state of life.

Adults fail in love toward their aged parents by refusing money for their support, by refusing to help them when they are in need, by neglecting to visit them or to console them in their loneliness, by neglecting to obtain the Sacraments of the

Church for them when they cannot go to church. These obligations may bind children under pain of serious sin.

3. The Fourth Commandment: The Obligation Of Parents To Their Children

Parents find the way to God and to family happiness by fulfilling the sublime duty of raising their children in the fear and love of God. Providing the necessities of life should not be a monotonous painful earthly task but a work filled with Christian joy.

Parents have the serious obligation of providing the necessary food, clothing and shelter for their children. Christian parents must give good example in a good Christian home. In the home there must be prayer and a spirit of love and cooperation. The parents should lead the children to the Eucharist and the Sacraments. Parents must provide a good moral and religious education for their loved ones. They must provide decent recreation and companionship.

4. The Fourth Commandment Offers Us A Christian Opportunity And Obligation To Serve Relatives, Friends And Members Of Our Community

Those close to us, our relatives and people living in our neighborhood should find us to be true friends. Christian affection and help to those near to us is our Christian opportunity and obligation. In serving others we serve the Christ Who was a friend to all.

5. The Fourth Commandment: Christian Love For Bishops and Priests

We serve God and His Church by fulfilling our obligations to honor, love, respect and obey the Pope as successor of St. Peter, our Bishop who is our shepherd and our priests ordained for our love and service.

> All should obey their bishop as Jesus Christ obeyed His Father; they should obey priests as if they were apostles. Let no one do anything touching the Church apart from the bishop. Where the bishop appears, there let the people be; just as where Jesus Christ is, there is the Catholic Church.
> Ignatius, Bishop of Antioch

6. The Fourth Commandment: Christian Obedience To Those In Authority In Government

All authority is from God. God is the Author of civil authority just as He is the Author of parental authority. We cannot today live good, decent lives and save our immortal souls without civil authority to rule us. Think what confusion and chaos we would have without public officials, policemen, judges, and so forth. You have a moral obligation to respect and obey the authorities of the city, state and federal governments. When the officials of these governments act within their power, it is a sin to show disrespect and disobedience. You must love your country, your state, and your city. You do this by helping the officials strive for material prosperity for all, for public health and education, for sound Christian morality and social justice. You must vote, pay your taxes, and pray for the rulers of the city, state and federal government. A good Christian serves his community and the needs of his community from love of God. No man is an island.

When there is a conflict between the law of God and the law of the government the law of God is to be obeyed.

CHRISTIAN PRACTICE

Lead your child to God by the force of your own example.

Make your home one in which God and religion are of the greatest importance. See that Christian decency in word and action is your ordinary way of life.

Lead your child in prayer by making prayer a daily habit in your home.

Keep out of your home the modern pagan attitudes and practices—indecent pictures and calendars, obscene, sensational or cheap magazines, books and comic books. Keep out of your home dangerous (immoral or cheap) radio and television shows.

Provide a Christian education for your child.

Lead the child to the Sacraments.

Give your child the right attitudes on marriage and family life.

Prudently encourage your child to be a priest, religious sister or brother.

CHRISTIAN PRAYER

O Lord Jesus Christ, You sanctified home life with untold virtues by being subject to Mary and Joseph. May they assist us to imitate the example of Your Holy Family, so that we may share with them their eternal happiness. *Feast of the Holy Family.*

O God, Your Divine Son, Jesus Christ, has shown us the way of perfect obedience by always doing Your will; teach us, Your Chosen People, to honor and love our parents, and to be obedient and kind to our superiors.

O Jesus, Your whole life was summed up in the words of St. Paul: *He humbled Himself, becoming obedient unto death, even to the death of the cross.* I, alas, have often rebelled against this important virtue, both by not observing Your direct commands, and by resisting the authority of those to whom You gave the right to command me. Permit me now to rebel no longer. Help me to see in those whom You have made my superiors the same Divine authority that You Yourself so faithfully obeyed. And if You will that I have any authority over others, grant that I may exercise it with the same gentleness, meekness, kindness, and unselfishness that were always evident in You.

SUGGESTED READING FROM SCRIPTURE

It devolves on sacred bishops who have the apostolic teaching, to give the faithful entrusted to them suitable instruction in the right use of the Divine books. *Second Vatican Council*

Lk 2:21-52 – Jesus' life at Nazareth.
Jn 6:35-40 – Christ came not to do His own will but the will of His Father.
Si 3:1-16 – Love your parents by obeying them.

Ex 21:15-17 – Death, the punishment of the Old Law for striking or cursing parents.
Si 3:1-16 – The care of old parents.
Col 3:20 – St. Peter told Christians to obey their parents.
Gn 44:1-34; 45:1-18 – Joseph's love for his brothers.
Ps 132:1-18 – How good where brothers live as one.
2 M 7:1-42 – The mother who would lose her son in death rather than see him sin.
1 Th 5:12-13 – Respect and love for those in authority over us.
Mt 16:18-19 – Peter the head of the Church.
Pr 4:1-9 – Listen to the wish of your parents.
Pr 6:20-35 – A father's advice to his son.
Pr 23:22-35 – Listen to your father.

Lesson 24: ASSISTING YOURSELF AND YOUR NEIGHBOR TO PRESERVE THE GIFT OF LIFE

1. The Gift Of Life

Natural life and existence are among God's greatest gifts to man. God gives this gift not only to you but to all other human beings. A Christian serves himself and his own needs by living a good healthy existence. A Christian serves his neighbor by helping him in all his necessities of body and mind. *By this love you have for one another, everyone will know that you are My disciples.* Jn 13:35. In serving yourself and the needs of your neighbor you are serving Christ because we are one in Christ.

> Just as a human body, though it is made up of many parts, is a single unit because all these parts, though many, make one body, so it is with Christ. In the one Spirit we were all baptized, Jews as well as Greeks, slaves as well as citizens, and one Spirit was given to us all to drink. 1 Co 12:12-13

2. The Fifth Commandment: You Shall Not Kill

The Fifth Commandment directs and commands you to care for your body, mind and soul and to care for the body and soul of your neighbor.

Your own life and your body are the means God gives you to serve Him, to serve yourself and to serve your neighbor. You must take care of your body, its life and health. Keep yourself clean, clothe yourself properly, obtain sufficient food and sleep, get enough fresh air and exercise, practice Christian self-discipline in the use of alcohol and tobacco.

You violate the Fifth Commandment by suicide of course. You violate the Fifth Commandment whenever you use alcohol excessively, or when you use narcotics to the detriment of your health. You sin by risking your life without sufficient reason. You sin by driving your automobile recklessly.

A Christian is obliged to train his mind to serve God, himself and others. School is necessary for a man to train himself for work in our modern society so that he can raise his family decently. Our Lord tells us of God's displeasure with the man who does not use the gifts God has given to him:

> It is like a man on his way abroad who summoned his servants and entrusted his property to them. To one he gave five talents, to another two, to a third one; each in proportion to his ability. Then he set out. The man who had received the five talents promptly went and traded with them and made five more. The man who had received two made two more in the same way. But the man who had received one went off and dug a hole in the ground and hid his master's money. Now a long time after, the master of those servants came back and went through his accounts with them. The man who had received five talents came forward bringing five more. "Sir," he said "you entrusted me with five talents; here are five more that I have made." His master said to him, "Well done, good and faithful servant; you have shown you can be faithful in small things, I will trust you with greater; come and join in your master's happiness." Next the man with the two talents came forward. "Sir," he said "you entrusted me with two talents; here are two more that I have made." His master said to him, "Well done, good and faithful servant; you have shown you can be faithful in small things, I will trust you with greater; come and join in your master's happiness." Last came forward the man who had the one talent. "Sir," said he "I had heard you were a hard man, reaping where you have not sown and gathering where you have not scattered; so I was afraid, and I went off and hid your talent in the ground. Here it is; it was yours, you have it back." But his master answered him, "You wicked and lazy servant! So you knew that I reap where I have not sown and gather where I have not scattered? Well then, you should have deposited my money with the bankers, and on my return I would have recovered my capital with interest. So now, take the talent from him and give it to the man who has the five talents. For to everyone who has will be given more, and he will have more than enough; but from the man who has not, even what he has will be taken away. As for this good-for-nothing servant, throw him out into the dark, where there will be weeping and grinding of teeth." Mt 25:14-30

A man must defend and protect himself against the worst type of murder—the loss of God's grace by serious sin. *What, then, will a man gain if he wins the whole world and ruins his life? Or what has a man to offer in exchange for his life?* Mt 16:26. He must guard himself against sin, especially serious sin, and anything that leads him into sin.

In very certain terms Christ tells us that we must care for other men and their needs:

> Then the King will say to those on His right hand, "Come, you whom My Father has blessed, take for your heritage the kingdom prepared for you since the foundation of the world. For I was hungry and you gave Me food; I was thirsty and you gave Me drink; I was a stranger and you made Me welcome; naked and you clothed Me, sick and you visited Me, in prison and you came to see Me." Then the virtuous will say to Him in reply, "Lord, when did we see You hungry and feed You; or thirsty and give You drink? When did we see You a stranger and make You welcome; naked and clothe You; sick or in prison and go to see You?" And the King will answer, "I tell you solemnly, in so far as you did this to one of the least of these brothers of Mine, you did it to Me." Next He will say to those on His left hand, "Go away from Me, with your curse upon you, to the eternal fire prepared for the devil and his angels. For I was hungry and you never gave Me food; I was thirsty and you never gave Me anything to drink: I was a stranger and you never made Me welcome, naked and you never clothed Me, sick and in prison and you never visited Me." Then it will be their turn to ask, "Lord, when did we see You hungry or thirsty, a stranger or naked, sick or in prison, and did not come to Your help?" Then He will answer, "I tell you solemnly, in so far as you neglected to do this to one of the least of these, you neglected to do it to me." And they will go away to eternal punishment, and the virtuous to eternal life. Mt 25:34-46

Besides providing for the needs of others as far as our resources will allow we must be careful not to injure the life or health of another unlawfully. Murder, which is the unjust killing of an innocent person, is a mortal sin; mercy killing and abortion are simply sins of murder. To cause injury by neglect of your property, to use excessive or unjust anger against your neighbor, to hate him, to fight with him unjustly are sins against the Fifth Commandment.

You are also directed and obliged in Christian teaching to care for the souls of others. We do this principally by practicing the spiritual works of mercy: to convert the sinner, to instruct the ignorant, to give advice to the doubtful, to comfort the sorrowful, to bear wrongs patiently, to forgive injuries, to pray for the living and the dead. You are your neighbor's keeper.

CHRISTIAN PRACTICE

Control your anger. Be like Christ Who was meek and humble of heart.

Practice charity toward people of other nations, races and religions.

Try to correct Christians guilty of national, racial or religious hatred.

Practice the corporal works of mercy: Feed the hungry, and give drink to the thirsty, clothe the naked, harbor the harborless, visit the sick, visit those in prison, bury the dead. Practice the spiritual works of mercy: Convert the sinner, instruct the ignorant, give advice to the doubtful, comfort the sorrowful, bear wrongs patiently, forgive injuries, pray for the living and the dead.

CHRISTIAN PRAYER

Pardon, O Lord, the faults which Your people have committed out of human weakness; and may Your loving-kindness deliver us from the entanglements of sin. Ps 35:1-6

For those afflicted in mind and body, for the poor, the sick, the dying and the persecuted, we pray to the Lord. *Prayer of the Faithful at Mass*

For those who are now in their last agony, that Mary, the Mother of God, will intercede for them, and St. Joseph, patron of the dying, will assist them, we pray to the Lord. *Prayer of the Faithful at Mass*

That our consciences be stirred to help the hungry and poor throughout the world, we pray to the Lord. *Prayer of the Faithful at Mass*

For those who show hatred toward us, that we may pray for them and do good to them, we pray to the Lord. *Prayer of the Faithful at Mass*

SUGGESTED READING FROM SCRIPTURE

Furthermore, editions of the Sacred Scriptures, provided with suitable comments, should be prepared also for the use of Non-Christians and adapted to their situation. *Second Vatican Council*

Gn 4:1-16 – God tells us of Cain's terrible sin of murdering his brother.
2 S 12:1-14 – God tells us how He punished David for the murder of Urias.
Mt 14:1-12 – God tells us of Herod's murder of St. John the Baptist.
Lv 19:17 – Do not hate your brother.
Pr 17:5 – Do not despise the needs of the poor.
1 Jn 2:9-11 – He that hates his brother lives in darkness.
1 Jn 4:20 – You cannot love God and hate your brother.
1 Jn 3:15 – Whoever hates his brother is a murderer.
Si 30:14-17 – The blessing of good health.
Mt 5:22 – God's punishment for unjust anger.
Rm 13:13 – Christians should live becomingly.
Ga 5:19-21 – St. Paul teaches the evil of drinking and carousing and the like.
Mt 18:7-8 – Leading another to spiritual murder.
2 M 6:24-28 – The aged Eleazar preferred death to scandal.

1. Chastity And A Christian's Consecration To Christ

The virtue of Christian chastity is the virtue by which a Christian regulates the use of his sexual powers according to the law of God.

A Christian consecrates his soul and body to Jesus Christ in Baptism. St. Paul reminds us of our consecration: *Keep away from fornication. All the other sins are committed outside the body; but to fornicate is to sin against your own body. Your body, you know, is the temple of the Holy Spirit, Who is in you since you received Him from God. You are not your own property; you have been bought and paid for. That is why you should use your body for the glory of God.* 1 Co 6:18-20. The Book of Wisdom tells of the joys of living chastely: *Oh how beautiful is the chaste generation with glory! For the memory thereof is immortal because it is known both with God and with men.* Ws 4:1-2. A Christian who violates chastity violates his dedication to Christ. *So then, my brothers, there is no necessity for us to obey our unspiritual selves or to live unspiritual lives. If you do live in that way, you are doomed to die; but if by the Spirit you put an end to the misdeeds of the body you will live.* Rm 8:12-13

God Himself created the first man and woman. Then, in order to people the earth, He (as it were), shared His creative powers with man. He gave Adam and Eve the command *Increase and multiply.* Gn 1:28. In order to accomplish this, He implanted in them a sacred power which we call the sex passion. It is something holy. It is something good in itself. It is something very important in God's plan of creation and providence. The misuse, the wrong use of this sex passion is what is evil.

2. The Sixth Commandment: You Shall Not Commit Adultery
The Ninth Commandment: You Shall Not Covet Your Neighbor's Wife

To preserve chastity a Christian, realizing his consecration to Christ, can help himself by praying frequently and fervently, receiving the Sacraments of Confession and Holy Communion frequently, having a great love and devotion toward Christ and

His Blessed Mother Mary, keeping his mind occupied with good things, avoiding places, persons and things that might lead him into sins of unchastity.

Christian parents should guard the chastity of their children. They should give the example of love of Mary, frequent prayers and reception of the Sacraments and should avoid unchaste conversations especially in the presence of children. Moreover, they should teach the child the facts of life tactfully, watch his books, companions and places of amusement. Teenagers especially need the parents' counsel concerning their dates, hours, education, companions and recreation.

Adultery is the sin of carnal intercourse between two people, one (or both) of whom is married. Fornication is the sin of carnal intercourse between two unmarried persons.

The full use of the sexual passion, i.e. sexual intercourse, is a right and privilege of those who are validly married. Therefore, adultery, fornication, masturbation and the fully deliberate desire of committing these acts are seriously wrong. Every Christian must heed the warnings of St. Paul:

> You know perfectly well that people who do wrong will not inherit the kingdom of God; people of immoral lives, idolaters, adulterers, catamites, sodomites, thieves, usurers, drunkards, slanderers and swindlers will never inherit the kingdom of God. These are the sort of people some of you were once, but now you have been washed clean, and sanctified, and justified through the name of the Lord Jesus Christ and through the Spirit of our God. Co 6:9-11

Christ said: *You have learned how it was said: You must not commit adultery. But I say this to you: If a man looks to a woman lustfully, he has already committed adultery with her in his heart.* Mt 5:28

Other acts which involve sexual passion between those who are not validly married (e.g. those keeping company) are at times morally good expressions of affection or at times venially sinful and even seriously sinful according to various circumstances: 1. the occasion of sin they might be to sins of adultery, fornication or masturbation (in act or desire), 2. the motives for which they are performed, 3. their duration, and 4. as is true of all sins, with what consciousness or deliberateness they are performed.

CHRISTIAN PRACTICE

Remember, you are in the presence of God Who sees everything.

Make friendships with decent people only.

Keep busy. An idle mind is the devil's workshop.

Keep away from bad companions and evil conversations, especially with people of the opposite sex.

Keep away from immoral books, magazines, newspapers, indecent shows, pictures, dances and anything else that might lead you to unchastity.

Pray fervently and frequently: "Mary most pure, pray for me." Receive the Sacraments of Confession and Holy Communion frequently.

CHRISTIAN PRAYER

Remember, O most gracious Virgin Mary, that never was it known that anyone, who fled to your protection, implored your help and sought your intercession was left unaided. Inspired with this confidence, I fly to you, O Virgin of virgins, my Mother. To you I come, before you I stand sinful and sorrowful. O Mother of the Word Incarnate, despise not my petitions, but in your mercy hear and answer me. Amen.

O sinless Jesus, Who said: "Blessed are the clean of heart, for they shall see God," grant me the grace of spotless chastity. . . . I am sorry for every sin and fault I have committed against purity in the past; for every undisciplined thought, for every evil word, for every impure action. I dedicate my future to the defense of the virtue of chastity, that my own soul may remain clean, and that Christian homes may be protected from the tragedies caused by impurity. O Mary, Virgin most pure, make my body pure and my soul holy.

SUGGESTED READING FROM SCRIPTURE

In this way, therefore, through the reading and study of the sacred books, let the word of the Lord run and be glorified. *Second Vatican Council*

1 Co 6:19-20 – Christians are temples of the Holy Spirit.
1 P 2:11 – Abstain from carnal desires.
Mt 5:27-28 – Lust in your heart.
Mk 14:38 – Watch and pray.
Rv 21:8 – Second death for the unchaste.
Gn 19:1-38 – The sin of Sodom and Gomorrah.
Ga 5:16-21 – Avoid the lusts of the flesh.
1 Co 6:9-10 – St. Peter warns the unchaste.
Ep 5:5 – Paul warns the Ephesians concerning unchastity.
Mt 5:8 – Christ's blessing for the clean of heart.

Lesson 26: CHRISTIAN OWNERSHIP

1. All The Goods Of This World Came From A Good God

God is a generous provider. He has put at the disposal of men more than enough of this world's goods. Moreover, a man must get a sufficient amount of this world's goods to lead a good Christian life and to raise his family in decent comfort. It is most difficult for a man to lead a good life and to raise his family virtuously without a sufficient amount of this world's goods—food, clothing, shelter, and money in the bank.

The material goods that God gives you are not for yourself alone. God gave them for yourself and for your family, but also that you may help others, especially those in need, to happiness here and hereafter. *If a man who was rich enough in this world's goods saw that one of his brothers was in need, but closed his heart to him, how could the love of God be living in him?* 1 Jn 3:17

2. The Seventh Commandment: You Shall Not Steal
The Tenth Commandment: You Shall Not Covet Your Neighbor's Goods

When a person realizes that all his possessions are from God and for God's purpose he must never be guilty of the sin of avarice. Avarice or greediness is an unchristian desire to obtain more of the goods of the world than are necessary for yourself and for your family. Never make the acquisition of wealth your main purpose in life. Destroy in your soul any instinct to greediness. One way to destroy greediness is to give generously to charitable organizations and to the Church.

To bring themselves closer to Christ by detaching themselves from the riches of the world some Catholics take a vow of poverty; the members of our religious communities in the Catholic Church give us a good example of the practice of the poverty of Christ. Christian poverty is a spirit of detachment from the goods of this world; it is not pauperism, or a lack of the necessities of life. Rich men can and should practice the spirit of Christian poverty. Many rich men do. Poor men with a spirit of greed in their hearts do not practice Christian poverty.

Mothers and fathers of families must use their money and their other material possessions for the well being of their families. The father and mother must understand that the money earned is for the family. They should never be guilty of wasting money. A family bank account is a Christian necessity. Parents must avoid poor management of family funds, foolish and unnecessary spending, foolish installment buying, running up charge accounts beyond their means, buying the children everything they ask for, the habit of borrowing, expensive drinking and gambling.

Gambling is not sinful in itself if there is no cheating, if everyone in the game has some chance to win, and if each one in the game is not risking money needed for his family or for himself. Gambling is not advised because it can lead to sins of dishonesty, to the loss of money needed at home, to quarreling, uncharitableness and broken friendships.

By the Seventh and Tenth Commandments God forbids taking something that belongs to another against his reasonable wish. Stealing, depriving another of his money or property by deceiving him, fraud, deliberately damaging the property of another, not paying your just debts, not making a reasonable effort to find the owner of an article you have found, depriving a laborer of a just wage, wasting the time, money, or property of your employer, depriving your family of needed money by gambling, drinking or foolish spending are all violations of the Seventh Commandment.

Violations of the Seventh and Tenth Commandments are serious sins if serious damage is done. If the damage is not serious, the sin is venial.

CHRISTIAN PRACTICE

Look upon all your possessions as things God has only loaned to you for a time.

Train yourself and your children in Christian poverty.

Put greed out of your hearts and be content with whatever you have. Heb 13:5

Measure your alms by what you have; if you have much, give more; if you have little, give less, but do not be mean in giving alms. Tb 4:9

Never take the smallest article that does not belong to you.

Pay your employees a just wage.

Always make a reasonable effort to find the owner of an article you have found.

Don't steal from your employer by "loafing" on the job, by wasting materials, or by careless work.

Avoid "shady deals" and "chiseling."

Train your child to be perfectly honest and above-board with everyone.

CHRISTIAN PRAYER

O Lord Jesus Christ, You, the Savior of the world, became poor as an example to us; graciously give us, we pray, the spirit of detachment from worldly goods, so that we may share in Your Messianic feast in heaven.

O God, Who punished Judas for his crime and rewarded the good thief for his penitence, be merciful to us. Our Lord Jesus Christ in His passion gave each one recompense according to his deserts. May He deliver us from deceitfulness of our old selves and bestow on us the grace of His Resurrection.

SUGGESTED READING FROM SCRIPTURE

We may hope for a new surge of spiritual vitality from intensified veneration for God's Word, which lasts forever. *Second Vatican Council*

- Mt 19:16-30 – Jesus advised the life of poverty.
- Lk 1:46-55 – Christ was born in poverty.
- Lk 6:17-26 – Blessed are the poor in spirit.
- Lk 14:15-24 – The poor will be invited to the Messianic banquet.
- Lk 19:1-10 – Zacchaeus promised to return stolen money and give one-half of his possessions to the poor.

Lesson 27: THE CHRISTIAN USE OF GOD'S GIFT OF THE POWER OF SPEECH

1. God's Gift Of Speech

The gift of speech is one of the greatest gifts of God. Speech is an external sign of being human. Speech enables a man to praise God and communicate with other men. We realize how wonderful is the gift of speech when we associate with an unfortunate person who has lost it.

The ordinary daily use of speech should teach us how holy this gift is. Speech enables the mother to train her child, the teacher to instruct his pupils, the priest to give you the Word of God. Speech enables Christians to counsel and to console each other, to help the poor and the sinner.

You should use your tongue to assist a person in whatever way you are able to do so. Above all you should enhance his reputation before men by speaking of his good qualities.

The Sacred Scriptures tell us that a Christian cannot be perfect until he learns to bridle his tongue:

> The only man who could reach perfection would be someone who never said anything wrong—he would be able to control every part of himself. Once we put a bit into the horse's mouth, to make it do what we want, we have the whole animal under our control. Or think of the ships: no matter how big they are, even if a gale is driving them, the man at the helm can steer them anywhere he likes by controlling a tiny rudder. So is the tongue only a tiny part of the body, but it can proudly claim that it does great things. Think how small a flame can set fire to a huge forest; the tongue is a flame like that. Among all the parts of the body, the tongue is a whole wicked world in itself: it infects the whole body; catching fire itself from hell, it sets fire to the whole wheel of creation. Wild animals and birds, reptiles and fish can all be tamed by man, and often are; but nobody can tame the tongue—it is a pest that will not keep still, full of deadly poison. We use it to bless the Lord and Father, but we also use it to curse men who are made in God's image: the blessing and the curse come out of the same mouth. Jm 3:2-10

2. The Eighth Commandment: You Shall Not Bear False Witness Against Your Neighbor

Even people trying to follow Christ can and do commit sins

against the reputations of others. If serious harm is done the sin is serious. All Christians should heed the words of St. James:

> The only man who could reach perfection would be someone who never said anything wrong. . . . So is the tongue only a tiny part of the body, but it can proudly claim that it does great things. . . . Among all the parts of the body, the tongue is a whole wicked world in itself.

Revealing a person's hidden faults, gossiping about a person's known faults, exaggerating his faults, telling tales about him are ways of damaging a person's reputation. Christians must realize that while it is never permitted to tell a lie, it is usually not right to injure a person's reputation even by telling the truth about him. *A flood of words is never without its fault, he who has his lips controlled is a prudent man.* Pr 10:19. A man can lose his happiness, his friends, maybe even his business and family when he loses his reputation. *A good name is more desirable than great wealth, the respect of others is better than silver or gold.* Pr 22:1

By the careless use of your tongue you can cause harm to another's good name; you can even steal from him his good name.

> Good name in man and woman, is the jewel of their souls. Who steals my purse steals trash; 'tis something, nothing; 'twas mine, 'tis his and has been slave to thousands. But he that filches from me my good name, robs me of that which not enriches him, and makes me poor indeed. Othello, Act 3, Scene 3

A lie is speaking something you know is not the truth. *From now on, there must be no more lies: You must speak the truth to one another, since we are all parts of one another.* Ep 4:25. It is never permitted to tell a lie, because every lie is an abuse of a sacred power given to you by a generous God. Lies can start quarrels and discord; lies can separate friends.

CHRISTIAN PRACTICE

Always speak the truth even when it hurts.

Correct your children when they lie or gossip.

Remember that everyone knows a liar and will not trust him even when he tells the truth.

See that nothing but good is said about anyone in your home.

If you mean yes, you must say yes; if you mean no, say no. Jm 5:12

Why do you observe the splinter in your brother's eye and never notice the plank in your own? How dare you say to your brother, "Let me take the splinter out of your eye," when all the time there is a plank in your own? Mt 7:3-5

CHRISTIAN PRAYER

Save us, Yahweh! There are no devout men left, fidelity has vanished from mankind. All they do is lie to one another, flattering lips, talk from a double heart. May Yahweh slice off every flattering lip, each tongue so glib with boasts, those who say "In our tongue lies our strength, our lips have the advantage; who master us?" Ps 12:1-4

Break for us, O Lord, the bonds of sin, and mercifully turn away from us the punishment we have deserved.

God Whom I praise, break Your silence, now that the wicked and the false are both accusing me. They are defaming me, saying malicious things about me, attacking me for no reason. In return for my friendship, they denounce me, though all I had done was pray for them; they pay me back evil for kindness and hatred for friendship. Ps 109:1-5

SUGGESTED READING FROM SCRIPTURE

Holding fast to this deposit, the entire holy people united with their shepherds remain always steadfast in the teaching of the apostles. *Second Vatican Council*

Pr 26:18-28 – God is telling us that one who bears false witness against another commits serious sin and is not to be trusted.
Dn 13:1-63 – The elders bore false witness against chaste Susanna; God punished them for their deceit.
Mt 26:57-64 – False witnesses were brought against Christ at the time of His passion.
Jn 8:44 – Jesus called the devil the father of lies.
Pr 12:22 – Lies are an abomination to the Lord.
Jn 18:22-23 – At His trial Jesus said He spoke the truth.

Union With God Forever

Lesson 28: DEATH

1. The Christian Hope

The Christian hope is for eternal life in God. *This is the testimony: God has given us eternal life and this life is in His Son; anyone who has the Son has life, anyone who does not have the Son does not have life.* 1 Jn 5:11-12

2. Death Is Certain

Death's visits come into our lives frequently. Ever and again we are called upon to assist at the last rites of some relative or friend; it gradually becomes clear that even those nearest and dearest to us will be cut off from us by death. Then each one of us begins to realize that he, too, will soon die. *Well then, sin entered the world through one man, and through sin death, and thus death has spread through the whole human race because everyone has sinned.* Rm 5:12

You know neither the day nor the hour of your own death.

> So stay awake, because you do not know the day when your Master is coming. You may be quite sure of this that if the householder had known at what time of the night the burglar would come, he would have stayed awake and would not have allowed anyone to break through the wall of his house. Therefore, you too must stand ready because the Son of Man is coming at an hour you do not expect. Mt 24:42-44

St. Paul says: *Since you know very well that the Day of the Lord is going to come like a thief in the night.* 1 Th 5:2. St. Paul exhorts us to be ready always for God and eternity:

> Brothers, this is what I mean: our time is growing short. Those who have wives should live as though they had none, and those who mourn should live as though they had nothing to mourn for; those who are enjoying life should live as though there were nothing to laugh about; those whose life is buying things should live as though they had nothing of their own; and those who have to deal with the world should not become engrossed in it. I say this because the world as we know it is passing away. 1 Cor 7:29-31

Death is a separation of the soul from the body. At death the body *returns to the earth as it once came from it, and the breath to God Who gave it.* Qo 12:7

3. The Christian Attitude Toward Death

For the Christian death is not a perpetual and impenetrable blackout. It is not hopeless and unrelieved suffering. It is not a barrier separating the Christian from happiness; it is the gateway to God Who alone can give eternal happiness. For the Christian death should be a time of joy.

> We want you to be quite certain, brothers, about those who have died, to make sure that you do not grieve about them, like the other people who have no hope. We believe that Jesus died and rose again, and that it will be the same for those who have died in Jesus: God will bring them with Him. We can tell you this from the Lord's own teaching, that any of us who are left alive until the Lord's coming will not have any advantage over those who have died. At the trumpet of God, the voice of the archangel will call out the command and the Lord Himself will come down from heaven; those who have died in Christ will be the first to rise, and then those of us who are still alive will be taken up in the clouds, together with them, to meet the Lord in the air. So we shall stay with the Lord for ever. With such thoughts as these you should comfort one another. 1 Th 4:13-18

The truth about the death of a Christian is beautifully expressed in the Preface of the Mass for the dead: *The life of those who are faithful to You, O Lord, is not ended but only changed; and when this home of their earthly life decays, an eternal dwelling place is prepared for them in heaven.* Death for the Christian is victory: *When this perishable nature has put on imperishability and when this mortal nature has put on immortality, then the words of Scripture will come true: Death is swallowed up in victory. Death, where is your victory? Death, where is your sting?* 1 Co 15:54

4. The Resurrection Of The Dead

As Christ arose from the dead to be glorified, so Christians arise from the dead; their bodies will shine with the glory of Resurrection. *Do not be surprised at this, for the hour is coming when the dead will leave their graves at the sound of His voice: those who did good will rise again to life; and those who did evil, to condemnation.* Jn 5:28-30. After your resurrection from the dead, you will live in eternity with the same body and soul you have now. You will be you. *And if we are children we are heirs as well: heirs of God and coheirs with Christ, sharing His sufferings so as to share His glory.* Rm 8:17

5. Christ's Promise Of The Resurrection In The Liturgy

Christ's promise of the Resurrection is beautifully given to us in the new funeral rite in the Catholic Church. A vigilant attempt was made so to structure the rite that it moves toward a climax, from the wake beginning with the recognition of sorrow and loss, the meeting of the body at the church to tie in with Baptism, the Eucharistic Liturgy to relate the Eucharist to the life and death of the Christian, the Final Commendation as a fitting prelude to the procession from church marking the triumph over death, the final ceremony at the cemetery to look forward to the Resurrection. A harmonious balance had to be struck between the human sorrow and grief of the bereaved in their loss—and the quality of the consolation that had to be offered them in the light of Christ's promise of the Resurrection. The new rite attempts to emphasize the consolation offered in the light of Christ's promise of Resurrection, while respecting the human needs of the mourners.

At the wake hope in the Lord, petitions for forgiveness and peace, perpetual and eternal light are the keynotes.

On the day of the funeral Mass the body is met at the door of the church with holy water, white pall and paschal candle. Holy water is appropriate because it reminds the Christian of his Baptism. The paschal candle also reminds the Christian of his Baptism and incorporation in Christ. A white pall, the size of the casket-cover, reminiscent of the white baptismal robe and decorated with symbols of the risen Christ, is placed on the casket by the priest and the pallbearers. One of the prayers of the priest at the door of the church sets the tone of the entire service: *When we were baptized in Christ Jesus we were baptized in His death; in other words, when we were baptized, we went into the tomb with Him and joined Him in death, so that as Christ was raised from the dead by the Father's glory, we too might live a new life. If in union with Christ we have imitated His death, we should also imitate Him in His Resurrection.* Rm 6:3-5

In the Mass the new liturgy relates the death of the Christian to his Baptism and captures the note of Christ's triumph over death. Prayers that carry overtones of fear and gloom have been eliminated. The tone of the liturgy is perhaps well expressed in the prayer of the Mass: *O God, recalling the Resurrection of Your Son, our Lord Jesus, we gather today to remember* , *Your son* (*daughter*). *Give him* (*her*), *we beg, the life You have promised all who believe in You. Through Jesus Christ our Lord.*

The rite after Mass is no longer called Absolution but Final Commendation and Farewell. It relates our deliverance through the power of Christ's mysteries. The theme is: *I believe that my Redeemer lives and at the last day I shall rise from the dust. And in my flesh I shall see God, my Savior.*

At the cemetery we Christians are taught to look forward to the Resurrection: *Since it has pleased Almighty God to call back our brother (sister)* , *from this life to Himself, we commit his (her) body to the earth, that it may return to that from which it was made. Christ was the first to rise from the dead, and He will remake our imperfect bodies to be like His glorious body. Let us entrust our brother (sister) to the Lord that He may raise him (her) again at the last day and make him (her) one with the saints in His kingdom.*

6. Judgment

The fact that all will be judged by God is without doubt and without dispute. *Since men only die once, and after that, comes Judgment,* says St. Paul in the Epistle to the Hebrews 9:27.

In modern Theology the time, place and manner of Judgment might be in dispute. We are told that the passage concerning Judgment from Matthew 25:31-46 is written more to emphasize the necessity of love of neighbor than to tell us the scene of Judgment as it will really be. However, it is an excellent passage to lead the Christian soul to a better life and to the fact of Judgment.

> When the Son of Man comes in His glory, escorted by all the angels, then He will take His seat on His throne of glory. All the nations will be assembled before Him and He will separate men one from another as the shepherd separates sheep from goats. He will place the sheep on His right hand and the goats on His left. Then the King will say to those on His right

hand, "Come, you whom My Father has blessed, take for your heritage the kingdom prepared for you since the foundation of the world. For I was hungry and you gave Me food; I was thirsty and you gave Me drink; I was a stranger and you made Me welcome; naked and you clothed Me, sick and you visited Me, in prison and you came to see Me." Then the virtuous will say to Him in reply, "Lord, when did we see You hungry and feed You; or thirsty and give You drink? When did we see You a stranger and make You welcome; naked and clothe You; sick or in prison and go to see You?" And the King will answer, "I tell you solemnly in so far as you did this to one of the least of these brothers of Mine, you did it to Me." Next He will say to those on His left hand, "Go away from Me, with your curse upon you, to the eternal fire prepared for the devil and his angels. For I was hungry and you never gave Me food; I was thirsty and you never gave Me anything to drink; I was a stranger and you never made Me welcome, naked and you never clothed Me, sick and in prison and you never visited Me." Then it will be their turn to ask, "Lord, when did we see You hungry or thirsty, a stranger or naked, sick or in prison, and did not come to Your help?" Then He will answer, "I tell you solemnly, in so far as you neglected to do this to one of the least of these, you neglected to do it to Me." And they will go away to eternal punishment, and the virtuous to eternal life. Mt 25:31-46

7. Christians Should Pray For The Dead

The dead who have not yet entered heaven are called the Poor Souls because they cannot help themselves; their time of probation was finished at death. They seem to cry out to us in the words of Job: *Pity me, pity me, you, my friends, for the hand of God has struck me.* Jb 19:21. Because they are our brethren, we on earth should pray for them, offer to God our good works and sufferings for them, offer our works of love for others for them and offer Christ in the Sacrifice of the Mass for them. We should remember the anniversary of death of our loved ones so that we can offer Mass for them. Follow the example of our Church. In every Mass offered there are special prayers for the dead. *It is therefore a holy and wholesome thought to pray for the dead, that they may be loosed from sins.* 2 M 12:36

CHRISTIAN PRACTICE

I will walk in Yahweh's presence in the land of the living. Ps 116:9

For dust you are and to dust you shall return. Gn 3:19

So stay awake, because you do not know when the Master of the house is coming, evening, midnight, cockcrow, dawn; if He comes unexpectedly, He must not find you asleep. And what I say to you I say to all: Stay awake! Mk 13:35-37

Many die suddenly and unprovidedly, for the Son of Man will come at the hour when He is not looked for. Imitation of Christ, Book 1, Chapter 23

Death is swallowed up in victory. Death, where is your victory? Death, where is your sting? 1 Co 15:55

Since men only die once, and after that comes Judgment. Heb 9:27

This I know: that my Avenger lives, and He, the Last, will take His stand on earth. After my awaking, He will set me close to Him, and from my flesh I shall look on God. Jb 19:25-26

For the Father judges no one; He has entrusted all Judgment to the Son. Jn 5:22

So I tell you this, that for every unfounded word men utter they will answer on Judgment Day. Mt 12:36

CHRISTIAN PRAYER

Blessed be the God and Father of our Lord Jesus Christ, a gentle Father and the God of all consolation, Who comforts us in all our sorrows, so that we can offer others in their sorrows, the consolation that we have received from God ourselves. 2 Co 1:3-4

Father, You loved the world so much that You gave Your only Son as our Redeemer. We ask Your merciful love for Your servant. Through the death of Jesus, You opened the gates of life to those who believe in Him. Do not permit our brother (sister) to be parted from You, but by Your glorious power, grant him (her) a place of light, joy and peace. New Funeral Rite

Now that we have been comforted by God's holy Word, let us pray for all the faithful departed, that they may be found worthy of the promises of Christ. Let us pray also for ourselves and for all Christians who are a living witness to the risen Christ and of mankind's victory over sin and death. *New Funeral Rite*

SUGGESTED READING FROM SCRIPTURE

It is clear, therefore, that Sacred Tradition, Sacred Scripture, and the teaching authority of the Church, in accord with God's most wise design, are so linked and joined together that one cannot stand without the others, and that all together and each in its own way under the action of the one Holy Spirit contribute effectively to the Salvation of souls. *Second Vatican Council*

Gn 3:1-19 – All must die because of sin.
1 Co 15:12-21 – The Resurrection of Christ is our assurance that we will rise on the Last Day.
Mt 25:1-13 – In the story of the Ten Virgins Christ tells us we must always be prepared for the great Judge Who will call us at death.
2 S:14:14 – All will die.
Si 40:11 – All things that are dead shall return to the earth again.
Lk 12:16-20 – Lay not up for yourself treasures on earth.
Rv 3:3 – I shall come to you like a thief, without telling you at what hour to expect Me.
Lk 20:27-40 – Through Jesus Christ the just will rise and die no more.
Zp 1:14-18 – Judgment Day is a day of distress and darkness for the wicked.
Mt 25:31-46 – Christ, the Judge, on the Last Day will separate the good from the evil.
Is 11:1-5 – Isaiah foretold that God will send a Judge who is just and merciful.
2 Tm 4:1-8 – Christ will judge us according to our deeds at the end of the world.
1 Co 3:13 – At the Judgment every man's work shall be manifest.
Lk 21:34-36 – Do not be filled with pleasure and care because Judgment Day will come upon you suddenly.

Lesson 29: CHRIST GIVES EVERLASTING JOY IN HEAVEN

1. Perfect Union With God Forever

The greatest joy in heaven is union with God for all eternity. Perfect unending union with the God of Salvation is the lot of those who maintained their union with Him in grace here on earth. *All we know is, that when it is revealed, we shall be like Him because we shall see Him as He really is.* 1 Jn 3:2. The joy of heaven is so great and mysterious that we on earth cannot even imagine what it is: *The things that no eye has seen and no ear has heard, things beyond the mind of man, all that God has prepared for those who love Him.* 1 Co 2:9

2. No Unhappiness In Heaven

The blessed in heaven are so united with God that they will have none of the unhappiness we experience on earth. *He will wipe away all tears from their eyes; there will be no more death, and no more mourning or sadness. The world of the past has gone.* Rv 21:4. The blessed in heaven will have as their companions Christ, the Man-God, the Blessed Virgin Mary, the saints and angels; they will experience great joy and see the heavenly condition of their own souls and body; they will enjoy the company of their family, relatives and friends, who are in heaven; they will know and understand many things which were puzzling to them on earth.

Anyone who dies in the grace of God free from all sins and free from the punishment due to sin goes immediately into the presence of God in heaven.

3. Prepare For Heaven

To prepare for heaven you should realize what it means to be a Christian and thereby unite your life with Christ in the love and service of God and men according to the teaching of Christ and the Catholic Church.

4. Purgation Of The Dead Before Entering Heaven

Many who follow Christ on earth and die in His grace need purgation or purification before entering heaven. Scripture reminds us of the necessity of purification: *Nothing unclean may come into it: no one who does what is loathsome or false.* Rv 21:27. Would any of us feel he is ready for heaven just as he is?

We cannot teach the time, the place and the manner of purification because it is not revealed to us. We do not know the length of time for the purification or purgation process for each person. It depends on the man's life and the mercy of God. We do know that we can help the dead by our prayers.

5. Christians Who Are Excluded From Heaven

The only people who are excluded from heaven are those who reached a state of cold obstinacy or complete rejection of God while on earth. They became impervious to God's love, mercy, forgiveness and God's desire for reunion with them. In short they are those who went to God in death and judgment in a state of mortal sin.

God's Word removes any doubt about the existence of hell. When Christ warns us to avoid temptation, He warns us of hell:

> And if your hand should cause you to sin, cut it off; it is better for you to enter into life crippled, than to have two hands and go to hell, into the fire that cannot be put out. And if your foot should cause you to sin, cut it off; it is better for you to enter into life lame, than to have two feet and be thrown into hell. And if your eye should cause you to sin, tear it out; it is better for you to enter into the kingdom of God with one eye, than to have two eyes and be thrown into hell. Mk 9:43-47

In telling us to stay away from people who can lead us into sin Christ tells us of the reality of hell: *Do not be afraid of those who kill the body but cannot kill the soul; fear him rather who can destroy both body and soul in hell.* Mt 10:28

The greatest pain in hell is to be separated from God forever. *Go away from me, with your curse upon you, to the eternal fire prepared for the devil and his angels.* Mt 25:41

It is very difficult to understand how the God of Salvation Who sent His Son to redeem us could place any of His sons in hell forever. However, God is not only good; He is also just. He must reward the good and punish the wicked. Those in hell refused to break their relationship with serious sin, thereby severing their union with God. They refused the grace of the God of Salvation and His Son, Jesus Christ, Our Lord.

We should beware not only of sin, but the habits of serious sin we can easily fall into today. A man who commits deliberate serious sin puts himself in danger. Serious sin can lead to a habit of serious sin and even total and eternal rejection of God's love. Serious unrepented negligence of your obligations to your marriage and family can lead to hell. Some violations of the law of love of neighbors are serious sins. Habits of unchastity are rife today. Serious violations of the laws of God and His Church are commonplace.

6. The Message Of Salvation

St. John tells of God's love for you:

> Yes, God loved the world so much that He gave His only Son, so that everyone who believes in Him may not be lost but may have eternal life. For God sent His Son into the world not to condemn the world, but so that through Him the world might be saved. No one who believes in Him will be condemned; but whoever refuses to believe is condemned already, because he has refused to believe in the name of God's only Son. Jn 3:16-18

God created the heaven, the earth and all things for you. God gives you His Divine life in Baptism. God brought His Revelation to the Chosen People so that you would receive His Message of Salvation presented in this book.

For you Jesus Christ His Son came with His teaching, His forgiveness and His grace. For you Christ died on the cross, arose and ascended into heaven. For you Christ comes in the Sacrifice of the Mass and the liturgy. For you is His fullness in the Catholic Church, His saving message, His Sacraments, His commandments.

For you is life eternal with Him forever.

CHRISTIAN PRACTICE

Fight the good fight of the faith and win for yourself the eternal life to which you were called. 1 Tm 6:12

We are waiting in hope for the blessing which will come with the appearing of the glory of our great God and Savior Christ Jesus. Tt 2:13

Prepare for heaven by placing the things of this world in their rightful place so that you will use them for the glory of God and the good of your neighbor. Spend your life in prayer and good works according to the laws and exhortations of God and the Catholic Church.

CHRISTIAN PRAYER

May the passion of our Lord Jesus Christ, the merits of the Blessed Virgin Mary and of all the saints, and also whatever good you do and evil you endure be cause for the remission of your sins, the increase of grace, and the reward of everlasting life. Amen. *Prayer after Confession*

O Lord, we implore You to grant this mercy to Your dead servant, that he who held fast to Your will by his intentions, may not receive punishment in return for his deeds; so that, as the true faith united him with the throng of the faithful on earth, Your mercy may unite him with the company of the choirs of angels in heaven. Through Christ our Lord. Amen. *Prayer on the Day of Burial*

O God, Who freely gives pardon, desiring the Salvation of mankind, we implore You in Your goodness to grant that our brethren, relatives, and benefactors who have left this world, may, by the intercession of Blessed Mary and of all the saints, share everlasting happiness in union with all the blessed. Through Christ our Lord. Amen. *Prayer at the grave on the Day of Burial*

SUGGESTED READING FROM SCRIPTURE

Those Divinely revealed realities which are contained and presented in Sacred Scripture . . . are sacred and canonical because, having been written under the inspiration of the Holy Spirit they have God as their author. *Second Vatican Council*

1 Co 13:9-12 – Union with God in heaven.
1 Jn 3:2 – In heaven we shall be like God.
Rv 7:9-15 – People from many nations are in heaven.
Rv 22:3-4 – We shall see God in heaven.
Ps 16:5-11 – The delights of heaven.
Is 25:8-9; Rv 21:3-4 – No tears in heaven.
Is 29:18 – In heaven the deaf will hear, the blind will see.
Is 35:5-10 – All joy, no mourning in heaven.
2 Th 1:6-10 – We shall see Jesus in heaven.
Mt 25:46 – Heaven will be everlasting.
2 Co 5:1; Heb 13:14 – Heaven our eternal home.
Ph 1:21-23 – To live is Christ; to die is gain.
2 M 12:43-46 – It is a holy and wholesome thought to pray for the dead.

THE COMMANDMENTS OF GOD

1. I am Yahweh your God. You shall have no gods except Me.
2. You shall not utter the name of Yahweh your God to misuse it.
3. Remember the sabbath day and keep it holy.
4. Honor your father and your mother.
5. You shall not kill.
6. You shall not commit adultery.
7. You shall not steal.
8. You shall not bear false witness against your neighbor.
9. You shall not covet your neighbor's wife.
10. You shall not covet your neighbor's house.

THE PRINCIPAL COMMANDMENTS OR LAWS OF THE CATHOLIC CHURCH

1. Assist at Mass every Sunday and Holy Day of Obligation.
2. Fast and abstain on the days appointed.
3. Receive Holy Communion during the Easter time.
4. Confess at least once a year.
5. Contribute to the support of your parish church and school.
6. Observe the laws of the Catholic Church regarding marriage.

PRAYERS

The Sign of the Cross

In the name of the Father, and of the Son, and of the Holy Spirit. Amen.

The Lord's Prayer

Our Father, Who art in heaven, hallowed be Thy name, Thy kingdom come, Thy will be done on earth as it is in heaven. Give us this day our daily bread and forgive us our trespasses as we forgive those who trespass against us, and lead us not into temptation. But deliver us from evil. Amen.

The Hail Mary

Hail Mary, full of grace! The Lord is with you: blessed are you among women, and blessed is the fruit of your womb, Jesus. Holy Mary, Mother of God, pray for us sinners, now and at the hour of our death. Amen.

The Act of Contrition

Oh my God, I am heartily sorry for having offended You, and I detest all my sins because I dread the loss of heaven, and the pains of hell, but most of all, because I have offended You, my God, Who are all good, and deserving of all my love. I firmly resolve, with the help of Your grace, to confess my sins, to do penance, and to amend my life. Amen.

The Apostles' Creed

I believe in God, the Father Almighty, Creator of heaven and earth; and in Jesus Christ, His only Son, our Lord: Who was conceived by the Holy Spirit, born of the Virgin Mary, suffered under Pontius Pilate, was crucified, died, and was buried. He descended into hell; the third day He arose again from the dead; He ascended into heaven, sits at the right hand of God, the Father Almighty; from thence He shall come to judge the living and the dead. I believe in the Holy Spirit, the holy Catholic Church, the communion of saints, the forgiveness of sins, the resurrection of the body, and life everlasting. Amen.